The Write P
Basics of Paragraph Writing

Kelly Kennedy-Isern

THOMSON

HEINLE

GLOBAL VILLAGE TORONTO
(The Language Workshop)
180 Bloor Street West, Suite 202
Toronto, Ontario
M5S 2V6 Canada

Australia Canada Mexico Singapore Spain United Kingdom United States

The Write Path
Basics of Paragraph Writing
Kelly Kennedy-Isern

Publisher: *Phyllis Dobbins*
Acquisitions Editor: *Kurk Gayle*
Marketing Strategist: *Jill Yuen*
Project Manager: *Angela Williams Urquhart*

Printed in the United States of America
2 3 4 5 6 7 8 9 10   06 05 04 03 02

For more information contact Heinle, 25 Thomson Place, Boston, MA 02210 USA,
or you can visit our Internet site at http://www.heinle.com

ISBN: 0-15-506519-X

Library of Congress Catalog Card Number: 00-111241

 **Contents**

1. Clauses:

The Independent Clause, The Dependent Clause,
Common Errors in Clauses   1

2. Sentence Structure:

The Simple Sentence, The Compound Sentence,
The Complex Sentence, Restrictive and Nonrestrictive Clauses   7

3. Prewriting:

Brainstorming, Clustering, Outlining   15

4. The Paragraph:

The Title, The Topic Sentence, Major Support, Minor Support,
The Conclusion Sentence, Timed Writing Assignments   21

5. Proofreading, Correcting, and Rewriting:

Proofreading, The Correction Process, Criteria for Graded
Writing Assignments, The Rewritten Paragraph   27

6. The Illustration/Example Paragraph:

Transition Words and Phrases   33

7. The Process/Narration Paragraph:

Transition Words and Phrases   37

8. The Classification Paragraph:

The Topic Sentence, Transition Words and Phrases,
The Conclusion Sentence   43

Contents

9.   The Descriptive Paragraph:
The Topic Sentence, Transition Words and Phrases,
The Conclusion Sentence   49

10.   The Definition Paragraph:
The Topic Sentence, Transition Words and Phrases,
The Conclusion Sentence   55

11.   The Comparison Paragraph:
The Topic Sentence, Transition Words and Phrases   61

12.   The Contrast Paragraph:
The Topic Sentence, Transition Words and Phrases   65

Answer Keys   71

Introduction

The Write Path is a basic course in paragraph writing for ESL students who have successfully completed a beginning-level and/or have tested into an intermediate-level ESL course. Students who plan to continue their education beyond ESL as well as those who need to improve their English for the workplace can benefit from **The Write Path**.

The Write Path offers fundamental instruction in constructing sentences as well as practice in organizing sentences to produce various types of paragraphs: illustration, process/narration, classification, descriptive, definition, comparison, and contrast. Students learn how to brainstorm, write outlines, and use a clustering technique to get started. The text includes a variety of authentic samples written by ESL students, stimulating exercises, and practical tips on how to develop effective paragraphs. In addition, it presents hints for how the teacher can make the class an inspiring writing workshop.

Students in **The Write Path** class will read authentic sample paragraphs written by ESL students similar to themselves who represent a variety of cultural and national backgrounds. Students will be able to relate closely to and learn from these samples, which contain typical errors as well as instructive corrections.

For many ESL students, not being able to write effectively in English is a hindrance to their future professional and educational goals. Although many of the students who will use **The Write Path** have some skill in writing paragraphs in English, many others at this level need practice in developing their basic writing skills. **The Write Path** addresses issues faced by both types of students. It gives lower-level students the tools they need to write effectively while it provides stronger intermediate students review and reinforcement activities as well as the opportunity to greatly improve their writing skills.

The Write Path provides various types of academic writing assignments as well as exercises that deal with grammar, style, and writing mechanics. Most of these activities can be introduced in any order that is appropriate to the immediate needs of the students. This flexibility promotes success as students get on **The Write Path** to becoming skilled writers.

Dedication

To my family for all of their support
To my sister, Jackie DuBosq, for her photos
To Ivonne Lamazares for leading me down the path of teaching
*To my husband, Kelly, for his encouragement, and for always
making me believe that I can accomplish anything*

Acknowledgments

To my colleagues at Miami-Dade Community College for their
valuable feedback on *The Write Path:* Leslie Biaggi, Isis Clemente,
Pattia Creelman, Myra Medina, and Susan Orlin. To Carol Call,
Nora Dawkins,
John McFarland, Hernando Marin, and Maria Vargas for piloting
The Write Path and sharing their valuable feedback.
To Ira Fernandez, Maria Jofré, Michelle Segall, and Dr. Cynthia
Schuemann for all their encouragement and support. To Dina
Forbes and Jacqueline Flamm at WordPlayers for their expert
advice and to Phyllis Dobbins, Michelle Pfifer, and my editor
Karen Eckardt-Gharib
for believing in this project from the beginning.

Chapter 1

Clauses

In this chapter, you will:
- learn how to write different types of clauses and use them effectively; and
- learn how to avoid making common errors in sentence structure.

At the end of this chapter, you will:
- practice identifying types of clauses;
- practice identifying common errors in sentence structure; and
- practice correcting common errors in sentence structure.

> A clause is a group of related words that contains a subject and a verb. It can also contain other words. Clauses are the building blocks of good writing because they are the basic elements of a sentence.

The Independent Clause

An independent clause is a clause that can stand on its own. It is a complete sentence. It expresses a complete thought.

An independent clause must contain:

- a subject   (Good **students** take notes carefully.)
- a complete verb   (Good students **take** notes carefully.)

It can contain:

- objects   (Good students take **notes** carefully.)
- modifiers   (**Good** students take notes **carefully**.)

A **compound sentence** is an independent clause that is joined to another independent clause by a coordinating conjunction (for example, *or, and,* or *but.* Turn to page 8 for a list of coordinating conjunctions).

A **complex sentence** is an independent clause combined with one or more dependent clauses.

- **Examples** •
  a. Linda's going to the store.   *(simple sentence)*
  b. Linda's going to the store, and Ricardo's going to the beach.
     (compound sentence)
  c. When Ricardo gets home, Linda will make dinner.   *(complex sentence)*

The Dependent Clause

A dependent clause is a clause that cannot stand on its own. It contains a subject and/or a verb, but it does not complete a thought. A dependent clause usually begins with a subordinating conjunction (for example, *when, because, while,* or *if*). It is not a complete sentence. Remember that a complete sentence must have both a subject and a verb, and it must form a comprehensive idea.

Each example below contains a dependent clause in a complex sentence.

> **• Examples •**
>
> a. While Bill was studying,   the phone rang.
>   *dependent clause*   *independent clause*
>
> b. I'll tell you   when I'm ready.
>   *independent clause*   *dependent clause*

The dependent clause in example **a** is not a complete sentence because it does not answer the question "What happened while Bill was studying?" However, combining the dependent clause with the independent clause forms a complete sentence.

When the dependent clause comes first in the sentence, use a comma after it.

> **• Examples •**
>
> a. After I went to the mall with my sister,   I went to the supermarket.
>   *dependent clause*   *independent clause*
>
> b. I'll go to the zoo   when my cousin visits me next month.
>   *independent clause*   *dependent clause*
>
> c. While I was studying,   my mother was baking cookies.
>   *dependent clause*   *independent clause*

  Now do Exercise 1 on page 5a.

Common Errors in Clauses

Read about some of the most common errors in sentence structure. All the examples given in this section are typical errors.

Error #1: The fragment

A sentence fragment, or fragment, is a group of words written as a sentence even though it is a dependent clause and/or lacks a subject or verb. A fragment can begin with a subordinating conjunction, as in example **a**. It can begin with a coordinating conjunction, as in example **b**. Some fragments do not contain a conjunction, as in example **c**. Also, most fragments lack a subject or verb.

• Examples •

Incorrect

a. *After we met them.

b. *And he lives in Miami.

c. *A man about six feet tall.

Correct

a. After we met them, we became great friends.

b. Her brother's name is Steve, and he lives in Miami.

c. A man about six feet tall entered the crowded room.

Error #2: The run-on sentence

A run-on sentence is a series of two or more sentences that are written as one sentence. Some run-on sentences can be corrected just by using correct punctuation and capitalization. For others, a conjunction must be added, and punctuation and capitalization might have to be changed also.

• Examples •

Incorrect

a. *I'm going to the library tonight I have to study.

b. *The happiest day of my life was when I came to the United States for the first time it was a dream come true.

c. *She loves to help people she always give me good advice.

Correct

a. I'm going to the library tonight because I have to study.
   (subordinating conjunction)

b. The happiest day of my life was when I came to the United States for the first time. It was a dream come true.   *(correct punctuation and capitalization only)*

c. She loves to help people, and she always gives me good advice.
   (coordinating conjunction)

---

*Throughout this book, an asterisk before a sentence indicates that the sentence is incorrect.

Error #3: The comma splice

A comma splice is similar to a run-on sentence. It contains two sentences that are incorrectly separated by a comma. To fix a comma splice, correct the punctuation and/or capitalization.

• **Examples** •

Incorrect

  a. *My favorite food is vegetable salad, it's easy to prepare.

  b. *It's easy to write the perfect paragraph, there are some simple rules that can help.

  c. *It's cold outside, you should wear a coat.

Correct

  a. My favorite food is vegetable salad. It's easy to prepare.

  b. It's easy to write the perfect paragraph. There are some simple rules that can help.

  c. It's cold outside. You should wear a coat.

 Now do Exercise 2 on page 5b, Exercise 3 on page 5c, and Exercise 4 on page 5d.

Professor _____   **Chapter 1/Exercise 1**

Name _____   **Date** _____

Underline each independent clause. Circle each dependent clause. Some sentences do not contain a dependent clause, and some sentences contain two clauses.

1. When John gets home, he'll make a telephone call.

2. Anton goes to school on Mondays, Wednesdays, and Fridays.

3. After Marie went swimming, she was hungry.

4. Erin loves spring, but she hates summer.

5. Don't go to sleep until you call your brother.

6. The teacher is here.

7. Mr. Baptiste sings and dances.

8. The girls next door are coming to our party.

9. Jim's trying to save money because he's flying to Switzerland next summer.

10. Cats are great pets, and they're easy to take care of.

11. Jay's leaving for California on Thursday, and he's returning on Tuesday.

12. Gail threw an anniversary party for her parents.

Score _____

Professor _____   **Chapter 1/Exercise 2**

Name _____   **Date** _____

Write **F** on the line next to each fragment. Write **R** on the line next to each run-on sentence. Write **C** on the line next to each comma splice. Write ✔ on the line if there are no errors.

1. _____ Mackenzie goes to bed at 11:00 every night, he wakes up at 7:00.

2. _____ While Chris was playing with his new computer.

3. _____ Mark bought a dog Karla bought new shoes.

4. _____ Carol loves to bake, but she doesn't have much time.

5. _____ Buddy takes care of the children, Janice works.

6. _____ When my husband buys me flowers.

7. _____ Although he gave Matthew money for lunch.

8. _____ The dogs were playing in the yard.

9. _____ Elisa loves to go to North Carolina in the winter Ed always goes with her.

10. _____ Mariana likes to go to the aquarium.

11. _____ Felipe turned in his assignment late, he got a bad grade.

12. _____ Did you enjoy the movie I did.

Score _____

Professor _____   **Chapter 1/Exercise 3**

Name _____   **Date** _____

Write ✔ on the line if there are no errors. Write **X** on the line if there is at least one error. Then write the sentence correctly on the line below it.

1. _____   My bedroom has a large dresser. With a mirror.

   _____

2. _____   Elena and David took their daughter Sara to a restaurant last night.

   _____

3. _____   Robert's band is playing tonight at the Warehouse Café, all his friends are going there to watch him.

   _____

4. _____   Because she was working on a new project. Louise worked late in her office last night.

   _____

5. _____   My classmate Denise is a very nice person. She's my friend. ·

   _____

6. _____   Dan and Kate rented a movie last night it was their favorite.

   _____

Score _____

Professor _____   **Chapter 1/Exercise 4**

Name _____   **Date** _____

A. Write two independent clauses.

   1. _____

   2. _____

B. Write two dependent clauses.

   1. _____

   2. _____

C. Write a fragment on the first line. Then make it into a complete sentence and write it on the second line.

   1. _____

   2. _____

D. Write a run-on sentence on the first line. Then make it into a complete sentence and write it on the second line.

   1. _____

   2. _____

E. Write a comma splice. Then make it into a complete sentence and write it on the second line.

   1. _____

   2. _____

Score _____

Chapter 2

Sentence Structure

In this chapter, you will:
- learn about the structures of different types of sentences.

At the end of the chapter, you will:
- practice identifying sentence types;
- practice using conjunctions;
- practice writing complex sentences;
- practice writing compound sentences with coordinating conjunctions; and
- practice using commas with nonrestrictive clauses.

> It is important to use a variety of sentence types to prevent writing from becoming boring and repetitive. Using sentence variety also demonstrates how you have progressed from beginning writing classes, where all you had to do was write correct simple sentences.

The Simple Sentence

The simple sentence contains a subject and a verb. It is different from other sentence types because it expresses only one complete idea.

A simple sentence can also contain complements and objects, and it can contain a compound subject and/or a compound verb.

• **Examples** •

a. The student   watched   the video.
   subject   *verb*   *object*
   (singular)

b. My cousins   sailed   in their new boat.
   subject   *verb*   *prepositional*
   (plural)   *phrase*

c. Gabriella and Ian   screamed and shouted   in the hallway.
   subject   *verb*   *prepositional*
   (compound)   *(compound)*   *phrase*

The Compound Sentence

The compound sentence consists of two independent clauses connected by a coordinating conjunction.

Use the acronym **fan boys** to remember the coordinating conjunctions: *for*, *and*, *nor*, *but*, *or*, *yet*, and *so*.

The examples below contain coordinating conjunctions.

• **Examples** •

a. Leslie went in the pool, **and** Patty sat in the sun.

b. Michelle and Bernie wanted to play tennis, **but** it was raining.

   c. The boy's grades were poor, **yet** he was allowed to take the trip.

   d. Larry won the lottery, **so** he quit his job.

   e. Peggy was working hard, **for** she had to finish her project.

   f. Robert didn't want to go to the ballet, **nor** did he want to attend the opera.

   g. Eddie might go to Disney World, **or** he might go to Sea World.

- Use a comma before each coordinating conjunction.
- In sentences that contain the conjunction *nor*, use the words in the second clause in the same order as in a question (as in example **f**).
- Remember that there is an independent clause on each side of the coordinating conjunction. Each of the clauses could stand alone as a single idea if the conjunction were removed and if correct punctuation and capitalization were used.

 Now do Exercise 1 on page 13a.

The Complex Sentence

The complex sentence is made up of one or more dependent clauses and one independent clause. The clauses are joined by subordinating conjunctions.

The examples below contain subordinating conjunctions.

- **Examples** •
  - a. Stephan and Ana went to school **after** they ate breakfast.
  - b. We brushed our teeth **before** we went to bed.
  - c. She left for work **when** the clock struck seven.
  - d. He went to the store **while** she cleaned the house.
  - e. I finished my composition last night **because** it's due today.
  - f. I have lived here **since** I was a child.
  - g. I'll study for the test **if** I have to.
  - h. I won't study for the test **unless** I have to.
  - i. He was absent from school **although** he knows he shouldn't miss any classes.
  - j. John ate his dinner **as if** he had never eaten before.

k. Carol didn't quit her job **even though** she won the lottery.

l. I turned down the radio **so that** my sister could study.

m. Richard will grade papers **until** he's finished.

n. Call me **whenever** you need me.

o. I'll travel to Ireland and Italy as soon as I graduate.

Do not use a comma between the independent clause and the dependent clause when the independent clause comes first.

so, so that

There is a difference between the coordinating conjunction *so* and the subordinating conjunction *so that*. In most sentences, *so* can be used as a subordinating conjunction instead of *so that*, but it still functions as and has the same meaning as *in order that*. There is no comma before it, just as there is no comma before other subordinating conjunctions.

The two versions of example **l** from page 9 have exactly the same meaning.

• **Examples** •

a. I turned down the radio **so that** my sister could study.

b. I turned down the radio **so** my sister could study.

When *so* is used as a coordinating conjunction, indicating a direct result, there is a comma before it, just as there is a comma before other coordinating conjunctions.

• **Examples** •

a. My favorite movie was on last night, **so** I stayed home to watch it.

b. Paul got a raise, **so** he can afford to go on vacation this year.

while

When the subordinating conjunction *while* is used to mean *at the same time*, there is no comma before it, just as there is no comma before other subordinating conjunctions. When it is used to emphasize a contrast between two different points, there is a comma before it.

• **Examples** •

a. Jane mopped the floor **while** her husband vacuumed the carpet.
(*simultaneous actions*)

    b. Joe likes to go to the movies, **while** his wife prefers to rent videos. (*contrast*)

 Usually the dependent clause can occur at the beginning of the sentence. When it does, use a comma after it.

- **Examples** •
  - a. **After** they ate breakfast, Stephan and Ana went to school.
  - b. **Before** we went to bed, we brushed our teeth.
  - c. **When** the clock struck seven, she left for work.
  - d. **Whenever** you need me, call me.

 Now do Exercise 2 on page 13b, Exercise 3 on page 13c, and Exercise 4 on page 13d.

Restrictive and Nonrestrictive Clauses

A dependent clause can begin with a relative pronoun.

Look at the relative pronouns that can begin dependent clauses.
- **which** (used with things)
- **that** (used with people and things)
- **who** (used with people)
- **whom** (used with people)

The examples below contain relative pronouns in dependent clauses. In each of the examples, the dependent clause is a restrictive clause. A restrictive clause is a clause that is necessary to the main clause of the sentence that contains it. It is not set off by, or enclosed by, commas.

- **Examples** •
  - a. The 1999 film **which** won the most Academy Awards is *American Beauty*.
  - b. Charles likes TV shows **that** have a lot of action.
  - c. Miguel is the student **who** was born in Havana.
  - d. Miguel is the student **who(m)** Angela is dating.

Another type of dependent clause that begins with a relative pronoun is a nonrestrictive clause. A nonrestrictive clause is not necessary to the main clause of the sentence. Without the nonrestrictive clause, the sentence has basically the same meaning. Nonrestrictive clauses are set off by commas.

> • **Examples** •
>
> a. *American Beauty*, **which** won the most Academy Awards in 1999, stars Kevin Spacey.
>
> b. Miguel, **who** was born in Havana, is a third-year student.
>
> c. Miguel, **whom** Angela is dating, is a third-year student.

The examples below are the same as the examples above without the nonrestrictive clauses. The basic meaning of each sentence is the same.

> • **Examples** •
>
> a. *American Beauty* stars Kevin Spacey.
>
> b. Miguel is a third-year student.
>
> c. Miguel is a third-year student.

The relative pronoun *that* cannot begin nonrestrictive clauses. It is used only in restrictive clauses to refer to people or things.

> • **Examples** •
>
> a. The woman **that** called Ben last night was his sister.
>
> b. The cake **that** Jake baked is delicious.

The relative pronoun *that* can be the subject of a clause, as in example **a**. It can also be the object of a clause, as in example **b**.

The relative pronoun *which* is used in restrictive clauses and nonrestrictive clauses to refer to things only.

> • **Examples** •
>
> a. *War and Peace* is the classic novel **which** is my favorite book.   *(restrictive)*
>
> b. *War and Peace*, **which** Leo Tolstoy wrote, is a classic novel. *(nonrestrictive)*

The relative pronoun *which* can be the subject of a clause, as in example **a**. It can also be the object of a clause, as in example **b**.

The relative pronouns *who* and *whom* are used in restrictive clauses and nonrestrictive clauses to refer to people.

The relative pronoun *whom* is in the objective case, like the object pronouns *him* and *her*. It cannot be the subject of a clause.

> • **Examples** •
>   a. Abraham Lincoln is the president **whom** John Wilkes Booth assassinated. *(restrictive)*
>   b. Abraham Lincoln, **whom** John Wilkes Booth assassinated, was the sixteenth president.   *(nonrestrictive)*

The relative pronoun *who* is in the subjective case, like the subject pronouns *he* and *she*. In speech and in informal writing, it can be used instead of *whom*.

> • **Examples** •
>   a. The woman **who** called Ben last night is his sister.   *(restrictive)*
>   b. Martina, **who** called Ben last night, is his sister.   *(nonrestrictive)*
>   c. Olivia, **who(m)** Ben called this morning, is his girlfriend.   *(nonrestrictive)*

The relative pronoun *who* can be the subject of a clause, as in examples **a** and **b**. When *who* is used instead of *whom* in speech and informal writing, it can be the object of a clause, as in example **c**.

The examples below show sentences that contain nonrestrictive clauses. These sentences are incorrect because the nonrestrictive clause in each sentence is not set off by commas.

> • **Examples** •
>   a. *Abraham Lincoln **whom** *John Wilkes Booth shot* was the sixteenth president.
>   b. *Martina **who** called Ben last night is his sister.

 Now do Exercise 5 on page 13e, Exercise 6 on page 13f, and Exercise 7 on page 13g.

Professor _____   Chapter 2/Exercise 1

Name _____   **Date** _____

Combine each pair of sentences to create a compound sentence by using a coordinating conjunction. Use subject pronouns and object pronouns for the underlined words. Use each coordinating conjunction once.

1. The students must study for the test. <u>The students</u> will fail <u>the test</u>.

   _____

2. The lobster smells delicious. <u>The lobster</u> looks good, too.

   _____

3. The Hoffmans don't want to stay home for Christmas. <u>The Hoffmans don't want to travel far</u>.

   _____

4. Carl's in love with Gina. <u>Carl's</u> going to ask <u>Gina</u> to marry him.

   _____

5. Maria needs a vacation. <u>Maria</u> has been working very hard.

   _____

6. Henry doesn't want to go to the movies tonight. <u>Henry</u> doesn't want to rent a video.

   _____

Score _____

Professor _____   Chapter 2/Exercise 2

Name _____   **Date** _____

Write **S** on the line for each simple sentence, **CP** for each compound sentence, and **CX** for each complex sentence.

1. _____ Irene went to the party, but she didn't have a good time.

2. _____ Susan and Marty want to eat at an Italian or Greek restaurant.

3. _____ When Mary's shift at work is over, she'll go home.

4. _____ Floria will go to college until she graduates.

5. _____ Maria, Dennis, and Dan are going to California.

6. _____ Martin is going to Utah as soon as his classes are over.

7. _____ Mark, Janet, and the kids barbecued and swam all day.

8. _____ Eddie will study hard, for he must pass his final exam.

9. _____ Carrie is sweet-tempered, beautiful, and smart.

10. _____ Glenn doesn't like steak, nor does he enjoy hamburgers.

11. _____ Luis and Marcy are going to the movies even though they don't want to.

12. _____ Jimmy eats constantly, yet he never gains weight.

Score _____

Professor _____

Chapter 2/Exercise 3

Name _____

Date _____

Fill in each blank with an appropriate coordinating conjunction or subordinating conjunction listed in this chapter. Add commas where necessary. If the order of the dependent clause and the independent clause can be reversed, write the new sentence on the blank below the original sentence.

1. Tonight I'll go to your house _____ you can come to my house.

   _____

2. I always brush my teeth _____ I wake up in the morning.

   _____

3. Sam stayed in Hawaii an extra week _____ he was having lots of fun.

   _____

4. _____ Marty was taking a shower the phone rang.

   _____

5. You'll fail the test _____ you study very hard this week.

   _____

6. I want to eat chicken for dinner _____ I want to have cake for dessert.

7. John and his girlfriend will help you _____ they're your friends.

   _____

8. Steve didn't wash the dishes _____ he swept the floor.

   _____

Score _____

Professor _____   **Chapter 2/Exercise 4**

Name _____   **Date** _____

Write complex sentences. For each sentence, use the independent clause and a dependent clause that begins with the subordinating conjunction. You can use the independent clause at the beginning or at the end of the sentence.

1. (we want to throw a party)   (so that)

   _____

2. (you'll have to show your ticket and your passport)   (when)

   _____

3. (the dog will be fed by the neighbors)   (because)

   _____

4. (she'll wait for you)   (until)

   _____

5. (you'll pass the class)   (if)

   _____

6. (you want to get married)   (yet)

   _____

7. (we can go to the movies)   (as soon as)

   _____

8. (the letter carrier came with a package for you)   (while)

   _____

Score _____

Professor _____ **Chapter 2/Exercise 5**

Name _____ **Date** _____

Each of these sentences contains a nonrestrictive clause. Add commas where necessary in each one.

1. Ross who got a promotion last month also got a raise.

2. Many scientists are searching for a cure for cancer which is a common disease.

3. Hank likes to travel with Jill who is his wife.

4. Robert Browning whom Elizabeth Barrett married is a famous poet.

5. Samantha's favorite play is *Hamlet* which was written by William Shakespeare.

6. Steve who you met last night is my older brother.

7. Tony who is the best student in the class is from Chile.

8. Chip lives in Spring Valley which is a small town in Virginia.

9. Tom Hanks whom we saw on TV last night is an accomplished actor.

10. The Nile which is in Africa is the longest river in the world.

Score _____

Professor _____   **Chapter 2/Exercise 6**

Name _____   **Date** _____

A. Write two simple sentences.

   1. _____

      _____

   2. _____

      _____

B. Write two compound sentences.

   1. _____

      _____

   2. _____

      _____

C. Write two complex sentences.

   1. _____

      _____

   2. _____

      _____

Score _____

Professor _____   **Chapter 2/Exercise 7**

Name _____   **Date** _____

A. Write three sentences containing restrictive clauses with relative pronouns.

1. _____

   _____

2. _____

   _____

3. _____

   _____

B. Write three sentences containing nonrestrictive clauses with relative pronouns.

1. _____

   _____

2. _____

   _____

3. _____

   _____

Score _____

Chapter 3

Prewriting

In this chapter, you will:
- learn how to use three techniques of prewriting: brainstorming, clustering, and outlining. This will prepare you to write topic sentences, support sentences, and conclusion sentences in Chapter 4.

At the end of this chapter, you will:
- practice the three techniques of prewriting.

Prewriting is one of the most important steps that you can take. It helps you to organize your thoughts so that your topic and the sentences that support your topic are logical (make sense), are relevant (are related to one another), and are parallel (are similar in form and importance).

Brainstorming

Brainstorming involves making a list of ideas about your topic. When you brainstorm, you quickly list the first ideas that come to your mind. You do not worry about grammar, punctuation, or neatness.

These are the steps to brainstorming about the topic "My sister is my best friend."
  1. Write down any ideas that you have about your topic (you can even draw pictures!).
  2. After you reread your ideas, delete any ideas that don't support the topic and combine any ideas that can be grouped together.
  3. Rewrite the ideas neatly and, for process/narration paragraphs, in a logical order.

Look at the example of the first step to brainstorming.

> • **Example** •
>
> *support each other*
>
> *likes to play tennis*
>
> *has good sense of humor*
>
> *reads similar books*
>
> *funny*

This example of the first step in the brainstorming process lists several ideas. The second step is to delete any ideas that are listed more than once and to combine similar ideas. Notice that *funny* can be deleted because it means the same as *has good sense of humor*. Also, *likes to play tennis* and *reads similar books* can be combined as a more specific idea: has common interests. None of the other ideas can be deleted or combined, so you can proceed to step 3: rewriting the ideas and, for process/narration paragraphs, putting them in order. After you finish brainstorming, it should be easy to write a sentence that states your topic.

• Example •

Topic: My sister is my best friend.

1. She and I have common interests.

2. She and I support each other.

3. She has a good sense of humor.

 Now do Exercise 1 on page 19a.

Clustering

Clustering is similar to brainstorming because it also involves quickly writing down ideas about your topic. The difference between clustering and brainstorming is the first step. Instead of writing the ideas in a list, you write them all over the piece of paper and draw lines to show how the ideas are connected. The second and third steps of clustering are the same as the second and third steps of brainstorming. Look at the example, which uses the same topic and ideas as the brainstorming example above.

• Example •

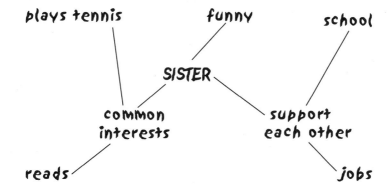

After you complete the first step of the clustering activity, you can proceed to the second and third steps, which would look like the continuation of the brainstorming example above.

 Now do Exercise 2 on page 19b.

Outlining

An outline builds on the ideas from the brainstorming activity. It consists of a sentence that states the topic, sentences that support the topic, and possibly a sentence that states a conclusion. You can add details more easily after you list the main points.

Look at the example, which uses the ideas from the brainstorming example.

• **Example** •

Topic Sentence: My sister is my best friend because she and I have common interests, we support each other, and she has a good sense of humor.

I.   She and I have common interests.

   A. We like to play tennis.

   B. We like to read and talk about similar types of books.

II. She and I support each other.

   A. She helps me with my schoolwork.

   B. We support each other with our jobs.

      1. I help her look for a job.

         a. I ask people to tell me if they hear of any employer who wants to hire someone.

         b. I remind her to buy the Sunday newspaper to look at employment ads.

         c. I take the bus with her and wait for her outside when she goes on job interviews.

      2. She encourages me when I have problems with my boss.

III. She has a good sense of humor.

A. She makes me smile even when I'm upset.

B. She laughs at funny things I say.

Notice that the sentences in the outline are parallel: When there is an A, there is a B; when there is a 1, there's a 2; and so on.

➡ Now do Exercise 3 on page 19c and Exercise 4 on page 19d.

Professor _____   **Chapter 3/Exercise 1**

Name _____   **Date** _____

Brainstorm one of the following topics. (In Exercise 2, you will write a clustering activity on one of the topics you do not use for this exercise.)

My most memorable day

Benefits of a college education

My favorite book

"Snail mail" vs. e-mail

Score _____

Professor _____   **Chapter 3/Exercise 2**

Name _____   **Date** _____

Write a clustering activity on one of the topics you did not use for Exercise 1.

Score _____

Professor _____   **Chapter 3/Exercise 3**

Name _____   **Date** _____

Fill in the blanks to complete the outline.

Topic: Discuss the differences between living alone and living with others.

Topic Sentence: _____

_____

I. One of the differences concerns expenses.

    A. _____

    B. _____

II. Another contrast is in the housekeeping chores.

    A. _____

    B. _____

III. _____

    A. You have more privacy if you live alone.

    B. If you live with others, you have to respect their rules.

Conclusion Sentence: _____

_____

Score _____

Professor _____   **Chapter 3/Exercise 4**

Name _____   **Date** _____

A. Think of a topic you have an opinion about. Write either a brainstorming activity or a clustering activity on it.

B. Now write an outline based on your brainstorming or clustering activity.

Score _____

Chapter 4

The Paragraph

In this chapter, you will:
- learn about the basic elements of a paragraph: the title, the topic sentence, major and minor support, and the conclusion sentence.

At the end of this chapter, you will:
- practice writing some of the basic elements of a paragraph.

Once you have learned how to write good sentences, you are ready for the next step: putting sentences together to write an effective paragraph.

The Title

There are many conflicting ideas about the use of titles. Instructors in some classes require a title, while others do not think that it is very important. A title is simply a way for you to draw interest and attention to your writing. A title should tell the reader in a word, phrase, or question what the composition is about.

A title can be very short, even only one or two words long (for example, "Smoking" or "Cigarette Smoking"); it can also be a longer phrase (for example, "Smoking: The Number One Killer" or "The Dangers of Smoking"). The title can even be a question (for example, "Does Smoking Kill?" or "How Does Smoking Kill?"). There are other ways that you can phrase a title, but the most important rule to follow is that the title should give a clear idea as to what the composition is about.

Each word in a title should be capitalized unless it is a coordinating conjunction (remember *fan boys*), an article (*a, an, the*), or a preposition (a word such as *in, on, through,* or *about* that describes a relationship between other words in a sentence). An exception to this rule is that every word, even if it is a coordinating conjunction, article, or preposition, should be capitalized if it is the first or last word in a title or subtitle—the part of the title that follows a colon (:).

The Topic Sentence

There are a few things to remember when writing a topic sentence. As you might guess, it should be a complete sentence. For this course, your topic sentence for most types of paragraphs should contain at least two main points. Look at the example of a topic sentence for each type of paragraph taught in subsequent chapters in this text.

> • **Examples** •
>
> a. <u>Illustration/Example Paragraph</u>
>   Dogs are good pets because they are loyal, entertaining, and protective.
>
> b. <u>Comparison Paragraph</u>
>   McDonald's and Wendy's are similar because of their prices, service, and types of food they serve.

    c. <u>Contrast Paragraph</u>
       Being married and being single are different because of freedom, money, and taxes.

    d. <u>Definition Paragraph</u>
       Computers are machines that can access, calculate, and process information.

    e. <u>Classification Paragraph</u>
       Animals can be classified into two groups: domestic and wild.

    f. <u>Process/Narration Paragraph</u>
       Making my first public speech was scary but exciting.

 Now do Exercise 1 on page 25a and Exercise 2 on page 25b.

Major Support

To use major support, write a general statement about one of the ideas from the topic sentence. The points of major support must be written in the same order as the ideas in the topic sentence. Each major support sentence should include a transition word or phrase to make the connection from topic sentence to conclusion sentence.

    • **Examples** •

    a. One reason New York is a wonderful place for vacation is the museums.

    b. The second way that a child can improve his or her grades is by rewriting the notes from class.

    c. Finally, computers are useful to solve difficult problems.

 Now do Exercise 3 on page 25c.

Minor Support

Minor support sentences give more specific information for major support sentences. A minor support sentence gives a detailed example to support what you are saying. For example, would you believe someone who said that women usually make less than what men with the same experience and education make at the same job? You might believe it, and you might not. However, if the person had some kind of proof, you might be more willing to believe it. That is the role of minor support. It makes what the writer wants to say more believable. To write minor support sentences, you can use transition words and phrases from the list on page 24.

- **Examples** •
  a. Women don't make as much money as men. Women are often discriminated against in the work place in regard to salary.
  b. Women don't make as much money as men. For instance, in 1997, a woman holding a full-time job earned 74.2 percent as much as a man holding a full-time job.

Notice that example **a** and example **b** have the same major support. However, example **b** gives a clear example that adds the element of truth that example **a** lacks.

Each idea of the major support should be followed by at least one or as many as three minor support sentences. Look at the examples of transition words and phrases that are often used in minor support sentences.

- **Examples** •
  a. *For example*, a parent can restrict television and playing privileges.
  b. *To illustrate*, books can be checked out at the library Monday through Saturday.
  c. *To demonstrate*, men can lift approximately twice as much as women.
  d. *To elaborate*, banks offer home loans, equity loans, and business loans.
  e. *Another example of this is* when cats spend hours cleaning themselves.
  f. *Another illustration of this is* that checking out books at the library is free.
  g. *Furthermore*, most of McDonald's Value Meals are priced under $6.00.

Examples **a**, **b**, **c**, and **d** can be used in the first minor support sentence. However, examples **e**, **f**, and **g** cannot be used in this position. They can be used only in minor support sentences after the first one.

  Now do Exercise 4 on page 25d.

The Conclusion Sentence

The conclusion sentence is the final sentence in a paragraph. This sentence is usually general, and it signals the reader that the paragraph is finished. It should be a restatement of the topic sentence.

• Examples •

a. In conclusion, having a brother or sister is good for many reasons.

b. In brief, having a brother or sister is good because you can share good times, help each other in bad times, and have someone trustworthy to talk to.

Notice that example **a** is very general, and example **b** is more detailed. Both examples are effective conclusion sentences. To write a more detailed conclusion sentence, like example **b**, find synonyms for the main words in the topic sentence and basically rewrite it.

• Examples •

Topic Sentence

a. McDonald's and Wendy's are similar because of their prices, service, and menus.

Conclusion Sentence

b. In summary, these two restaurants are alike because of the food costs, the employees' attitudes toward customers, and the types of food they have.

Example **b** uses the transition phrase *In summary*. Look at the examples of the same sentence with two other transition phrases that are often used in conclusion sentences.

• Examples •

a. In brief, these two restaurants are alike because of the food costs, the employees' attitudes toward customers, and the types of food served.

b. In conclusion, these two restaurants are alike because of the food costs, the employees' attitudes toward customers, and the types of food served.

Timed Writing Assignments

Timed writing assignments will make up the majority of the assignments in this course. To complete a timed writing assignment, you will write on a given topic for a specified amount of time. Your paragraph will be graded on a scale of 1 to 5. Then your paragraph will be returned to you and you will rewrite it for a second grade. (See Chapter 5 for information about the grading system and the rewriting process.)

 Now do Exercise 5 on page 25e.

Professor _____   **Chapter 4/Exercise 1**

Name _____   **Date** _____

Write a topic sentence for each idea.

1. Discuss the best way to choose a car.

   _____

2. Explain why it is smart to finish your education.

   _____

3. Define the perfect spouse.

   _____

4. Discuss the different types of students in your classroom.

   _____

5. Discuss the similarities between being married and being single.

   _____

6. Discuss the differences between being married and being single.

   _____

7. Explain why you enjoy your favorite hobby.

   _____

8. Discuss the advantages of exercising regularly.

   _____

Score _____

Professor _____   **Chapter 4/Exercise 2**

Name _____   **Date** _____

Circle the letter of the best topic sentence. Remember that a topic sentence should not be too narrow or too general.

1. a. Vacations are great.

   b. Vacations are nice because you can swim at the beach.

   c. Vacations are enjoyable because you can relax, spend time with your family, and visit interesting places.

2. a. The Honda Civic is an excellent car because of its low price.

   b. The Honda Civic is a good car because it is low-priced and dependable.

   c. The Honda Civic is my favorite car.

3. a. Computers are useful to process data, store information, and generate reports.

   b. Computers can help you to calculate complex data.

   c. Computers are useful machines.

4. a. Getting a college education can help you in your career.

   b. It is important to have a college degree.

   c. Having a college degree can help you personally and professionally.

Score _____

Professor _____   **Chapter 4/Exercise 3**

Name _____   **Date** _____

Write three major support sentences for each topic sentence.

1. Using public transportation is a good idea because it saves money, helps the environment, and is safer than traveling by car.

   Major support #1: _____

   _____

   Major support #2: _____

   _____

   Major support #3: _____

   _____

2. Adults and children differ in respect to their experience, health, and finances.

   Major support #1: _____

   _____

   Major support #2: _____

   _____

   Major support #3: _____

   _____

Score _____

Professor _____   **Chapter 4/Exercise 4**

Name _____   **Date** _____

Write a minor support sentence for each major support sentence.

1. Another reason people get divorced is infidelity.

_____

_____

2. The final reason cats are good pets is that you can leave them alone without supervision while you are on vacation.

_____

_____

3. Another step is to find a quiet place to study.

_____

_____

4. The perfect friend is also trustworthy.

_____

_____

5. In addition, the cruise was a chance for my husband and me to relax.

_____

_____

Score _____

Professor _____   **Chapter 4/Exercise 5**

Name _____   **Date** _____

Think of your own topic. Write one each of the following.

Title:

_____

Topic sentence:

_____

Major support:

_____

Minor support:

_____

Conclusion sentence:

_____

Score _____

Chapter 5

Proofreading, Correcting, and Rewriting

In this chapter, you will:
- learn how to proofread and correct your writing assignments to ensure that they exhibit the traits necessary to be considered good writing.

At the end of this chapter, you will:
- practice identifying and correcting errors in writing.

Writing must have several specific traits in order to be considered effective. Good writing demonstrates correct grammar, sentence structure, and mechanics such as punctuation, capitalization, and spelling. In addition, good writing expresses thoughts clearly and accurately.

Proofreading

Proofreading involves rereading a composition to look for mistakes. Typically, you should spend approximately five minutes proofreading a paragraph-length writing assignment.

Read the writing assignment backward (one sentence at a time) to make sure that each sentence is complete. This makes you focus on each sentence and its completeness.

Before submitting a writing assignment, ask yourself the following questions:
- Does each verb agree with each subject?
- Is each sentence a complete thought?
- Does each sentence contain a subject and a main verb?
- Is each sentence complete, including each of those beginning with an *–ing* verb?
- Have I used correct punctuation?
- Does my topic sentence contain at least one good idea?
- Does each idea in the topic sentence have both major and minor support?

The Correction Process

The correction process that you will be using in this class might be different from any process that you have used before. It involves your instructor using a number system to indicate your mistakes. In this way, you are responsible for making the actual correction; therefore, you will learn more effectively than you would if your instructor made the corrections. This process also enables you to receive two grades for each writing assignment: one for the rough draft and one for the rewritten version. The instructor will advise you of the weight of each assignment (how much the assignment counts toward your final grade for the course). Look at the correction system, which represents the most common errors.

Correction System

Grammar

1. subject-verb agreement
2. singular/plural usage
3. article usage
4. verb tense
5. verb form
6. word form
7. pronoun usage

Sentence Structure

8. fragment
9. run-on sentence
10. comma splice
11. word order

Word Choice

12. preposition use
13. wrong word or phrase

Paragraph

14. topic sentence
15. conclusion sentence
16. transition words and phrases
17. relevant support

Miscellaneous

18. spelling
19. capitalization
20. punctuation
21. omission/unnecessary word or phrase

Criteria for Graded Writing Assignments

Your instructor will use the following criteria to grade your writing assignments.

5

A writing assignment with this grade is equal to a writing assignment with the letter grade *A*. It has a clear topic sentence, and it directly addresses the topic. This writing assignment uses transition words correctly. It uses simple, compound, and complex sentences containing conjunctions such as *when, because, while, before,* and *after*. It has a few grammatical errors, but they do not interfere with the reader's understanding of the writing assignment. This writing assignment has no more than one fragment, run-on, or comma splice.

4

A writing assignment with this grade is above average. It contains a clear topic sentence, logical organization, and sufficient support. Transition words and phrases are used correctly, and correct punctuation is used. Agreement, tense, spelling, and possession are usually correct. Errors in usage, grammar, syntax, and mechanics do not interfere with the reader's understanding. This writing assignment contains a combination of simple, compound, and/or complex sentences. Ideally, it should have no more than one fragment, run-on, or comma splice.

3

A writing assignment with this grade is average. There is a topic sentence, but it might be too general or too specific. The writing assignment has support, but some ideas might be underdeveloped. Most transition words and phrases are used correctly. Errors in sentence structure, usage, and mechanics are not frequent and do not greatly affect readability. This writing assignment contains mostly simple sentences and a few compound and/or complex sentences. It has no more than two fragments, run-ons, or comma splices. A 3 is the lowest passing grade.

2

A writing assignment with this grade is below average. It has a topic sentence, but it is either unclear or too general. There is no clear pattern of organization. Several transition words and phrases (if present) are used incorrectly. It contains many of the errors listed above and lacks compound and/or complex sentences. This is not a passing grade.

1

A writing assignment with this grade is among the weakest. A writing assignment with this grade has no topic sentence and/or is unclear, and the pattern of organization and its connection to the topic might not be apparent. Errors listed above are so frequent that they seriously distract the reader. This is not a passing grade.

The Rewritten Paragraph

As discussed earlier, you will write each timed paragraph twice. The first time will be a rough draft. Your instructor will number the rough draft. Then you will decide what the mistakes are, figure out how to fix the problems, and rewrite the entire paragraph.

Look at the example, which contains several errors. With a partner, analyze each of the errors according to the correction system on page 29. Try to correct the errors. Then analyze the corrected example together.

Rough Draft

Aleida Fujita

The Happiest Time in My Life

The happiest time in my life was <u>the</u> last vacation in Cuba. It was <u>beatiful</u>,
                                    13   18

I played baseball with my family. I went to the park with my husband _ <u>her</u> father, and
                                                                        20 13

my children. <u>I went to the pool, I swam very fast in the pool.</u> My children played in the
                                    10

park with <u>others</u> children. They were very excited. They were playing until <u>Late</u> at
            6   19

<u>nigh</u>. I will never <u>forgot</u> <u>the</u> <u>Last</u> vacation in Cuba. <u>Was the best time in my life</u>.
18   4   13   19   8

Rewritten Paragraph

Aleida Fujita

The Happiest Time in My Life

The happiest time in my life was my last vacation in Cuba. It was beautiful. I

played baseball with my family. I went to the park with my husband, his father, and my

children. I went to the pool, and I swam very fast in the pool. My children played in the

park with the other children. They were very excited. They were playing until late at

night. I will never forget my last vacation in Cuba. It was the best time in my life.

   Now do Exercise 1 on page 31a.

Professor _____   **Chapter 5/Exercise 1**

Name _____   **Date** _____

Use the correction system on page 29 to correct the following rough draft of a paragraph. Then rewrite it. Skip lines when you write.

Williams Garcia

How to Get an A

I likes to get an A at class, but I need study every day. I often go to the library at night, that is how I prepare for class. I reads the newspaper every day. And grammar books before I go to sleep. I Listen to the radio or watch TV daily. I am speaking English with my friends in work and on bus.

_____

_____

_____

_____

_____

_____

_____

_____

_____

_____

Score _____

Chapter 6

The Illustration/Example Paragraph

In this chapter, you will:
- learn how to write and analyze illustration/example paragraphs.

At the end of the chapter, you will:
- practice using transition words and phrases correctly;
- practice writing support sentences;
- practice analyzing and correcting an illustration/example paragraph; and
- complete a timed writing assignment for an illustration/example paragraph.

This is Larisa Slatsnaya.
You will read her paragraph
on pages 34 and 35.

> The illustration paragraph, or example paragraph, demonstrates a writer's opinion about a subject. The writer uses concrete and detailed examples to show a point of view.

Transition Words and Phrases

There are certain transition words and phrases that are common to the illustration/example paragraph.

- **Examples** -
    a. ***First of all***, writing poetry helps me express my feelings.
    b. ***Secondly***, the lines are very long at the bank on Fridays.
    c. ***The first reason*** is that computers can calculate information very quickly.
    d. ***To illustrate***, most of McDonald's Value Meals are less than six dollars.
    e. ***To demonstrate***, Mr. Wirtel gives his students opportunities to do extra credit.

Notice that in examples **a**, **b**, **d**, and **e**, there is a comma after the transition word or phrase, followed by an independent clause. There is no comma in example **c**.

Look at the authentic student sample paragraph. Remember that this is a first draft. You will also see the numbers showing errors.

Larisa Slatsnaya

Factors that Increase the Divorce Rate

Incompatibility infidelity, and drug or alcohol problems are some of the most
20
common reasons that there is an increase in the number of people who get

divorce. First of all, incompatibility is a reasons for divorce. For example, people
6   2
who have an unrealistic view at married life will soon be disappointed when
12
they realize that to be married means not only to have romantic love, but

to also have family obligations. <u>And infidelity can poison family life.</u> For instance,
11   8

if the spouses don't have areas of shared contentment and do not unite with

common ideas of life_they will try to find all that is <u>necesary</u> for the soul and
20   18

the body with another person. Drug and alcohol problems are common factors in

life and have <u>destruct</u> roles. To illustrate, nobody wants to be the target of
6

love for the person who has immoral habits. In conclusion, <u>problem</u> such as
2

incompatibility, infidelity, and drug or alcohol abuse can be the cause of divorce.

Discussion Questions

1. Is Larisa's topic sentence complete? Explain.

   _____

2. List two ways that Larisa can improve her writing for her next assignment.

   a. _____

   b. _____

3. Are Larisa's minor support sentences effective examples? Why or why not?

   _____

   _____

4. Does Larisa's conclusion sentence sufficiently summarize her paragraph? Why or why not?

   _____

➡ Now do Exercises 1–4 on pages 35a–35d.

Professor _____   **Chapter 6/Exercise 1**

Name _____   **Date** _____

Fill in each blank with one of the following phrases. Use correct capitalization and punctuation.

the final reason	to illustrate	secondly	to demonstrate
the first reason	for example	in brief	

Miami is a great place for vacation because of the attractions, the

beaches, and the weather. _____ Miami is a

good vacation spot is the attractions. _____

Miami has the Seaquarium, Vizcaya, and Bayside Marketplace. _____

_____ Miami is a good vacation spot because of the

beaches. _____ Miami has white sand, blue

water, and beautiful palm trees. _____ _____

this vacation spot is wonderful is the weather. _____

the temperature is rarely under 70 degrees, and it's usually sunny.

_____ , Miami is a fantastic spot for vacation.

Score _____

Professor _____   **Chapter 6/Exercise 2**

Name _____   **Date** _____

Complete each of the following sentences. Add punctuation where necessary.

1. The second reason that a college education is important

   _____

   _____

2. Cats are also more independent. For example

   _____

   _____

3. Watching movies is a good way to learn English because you can hear correct pronunciation, learn new vocabulary, and talk about the movie with your friends. First

   _____

   _____

4. It's difficult to attend school while working because you don't have time to study. To illustrate

   _____

   _____

Score _____

Professor _____   **Chapter 6/Exercise 3**

Name _____   **Date** _____

Rewrite Larisa's paragraph on pages 34–35. Skip lines when you write.

_____
_____
_____
_____
_____
_____
_____
_____
_____
_____
_____
_____
_____
_____
_____
_____
_____
_____
_____
_____
_____
_____
_____

Score _____

Professor _____   **Chapter 6/Exercise 4**

Name _____   **Date** _____

Timed Writing Assignment

Write an illustration/example paragraph on one of the following topics. Write a title for your paragraph. Skip lines when you write. Use the back of the page if necessary.

Topic A: What are some of the reasons people change jobs?

Topic B: Detail the reasons that you think people who live in the United States should (or shouldn't) have to learn English.

Topic C: Explain why (name of movie) is your favorite movie.

Topic D: Explain some of the benefits of being married.

Topic E: Discuss some of the ways winning the lottery would change your life.

Topic F: Detail some of the reasons that computers are useful.

Topic G: Explain a few reasons that (name of car) is the best car to buy.

_____

_____

_____

_____

_____

_____

_____

_____

_____

_____

_____

_____

_____

_____

Score _____

Chapter 7

The Process/Narrative Paragraph

In this chapter, you will:
- learn how to write and analyze process/narrative paragraphs.

At the end of the chapter, you will:
- practice using transition words and phrases correctly;
- practice putting sentences of a process/narrative paragraph in the correct order; and
- complete a timed writing assignment for a process/narrative paragraph.

This is Wichai Tirasitipol, and to the right is Joy Maritana. You will read Wichai's paragraph on page 39 and Joy's paragraph on pages 40 and 41.

We use the process/narrative paragraph to show how something is usually done, describe the best way to do something, or tell a story. The process/narrative paragraph follows a step-by-step or chronological order. This type of paragraph is different from other types because minor support is not always necessary. To decide whether to use minor support, ask yourself, "Do I need an example to make this point clear?"

The Topic Sentence

If you are writing a process paragraph, you should demonstrate that the process being described is simple. If you are writing a narrative paragraph, you should clearly describe the main point of your story. In other words, describe why you are telling the story and why it is important. The topic sentences for both of these types of paragraphs are more general than the topic sentences for other types of paragraphs.

• Examples •

a. The first day of my job was exciting and scary.

b. Registering for classes at your local college is simple if you follow this advice.

c. The day my baby was born was the most wonderful day of my life.

d. Studying for a test is easy if you follow these directions.

Transition Words and Phrases

Some transition words and phrases are common to the process/narrative paragraph.

• Examples •

a. *First*, design an exercise plan that you can follow every week.

b. *Next*, add the flour and vanilla.

c. *After* that, my boyfriend asked me to marry him.

d. *Before* you register, you must see an advisor.

e. *During* the revision stage, errors in grammar, structure, and mechanics should be corrected.

f. *The second step* is to change the tires.

g. *Finally*, you should comb your dog's fur.

h. **While** one student rewrites the notes, another highlights the textbook.

i. **Then** Mr. Lorenzo bought us tickets for a Broadway play.

j. **Later (on)**, mop the floor with a good cleaning product.

━▶　Now do Exercise 1 on page 41a.

The two authentic student sample paragraphs in this chapter are different but have some distinctive features. Look at the authentic student paragraph. Remember that this is a first draft. You will also see the numbers showing the errors.

For extra credit, you can correctly rewrite the sample paragraph.

Wichai Tirasitipol

How to Plan a Birthday Party

Birthday parties <u>have</u> so much fun and a lot of friends come to my house, so
₁₃

I have <u>much</u> things to do. First of all, I have to estimate the number __ people that
₁₃　　　　　　　　　　　　　　　　　　　　　　　　　　₂₁

will be in my house. For example, I have to have <u>food enough</u> and plenty of <u>beverage</u>
₁₁　　　　　　　　　　　　₂

for all the guests. <u>Also, what day the party will be.</u> Second, I prepare the <u>thai</u>
₈　　　　　　　　　　　　　　　　　　₁₉

food, such as soup, appetizer, main course, wine, and beer. Finally, I check that my

camera still <u>work</u> and buy <u>films</u> before the party starts. <u>In</u> the party, it is good
₁　　　　　₂　　　　　　　　　　　　　　　₁₂

to take candid pictures. <u>In brief, I will have a good time I will be tired too.</u>
₉

Discussion Questions

1. Does Wichai use transition words and phrases correctly? _____
   Give three examples.

   a. _____   b. _____   c. _____

2. List two positive aspects of Wichai's paragraph.

   a. _____

   b. _____

3. List two ways that Wichai can improve his writing for his next paragraph.

   a. _____

   b. _____

Joy Maritana

The Happiest Day in My Life

The happiest day in my life was when I arrived in __ United States.
Three reasons are I was reunited with my mother, I had better educational
opportunities, and __ was exited about a new life in a new country. First of
all, the happiest day in my life was when I was reunited with my mom, about
eighth years ago. I miss her a lot when she is not around me growing up,

but __ most important thing is that Im with her now, and I'm happy to be
2/

with her. Second, I have better educational opportunities, I did not have
10

them in my country. Someday I would like to be a successful

Radiographer. And that is why this was the happiest day in my life.
19   8

Discussion Questions

1. How would you fix the comma splice in Joy's paragraph?

   _____

   _____

2. How would you rewrite Joy's conclusion sentence?

   _____

   _____

3. List two positive aspects of Joy's paragraph.

   a. _____

   b. _____

4. List two ways that Joy can improve her writing for her next paragraph.

   a. _____

   b. _____

➡ Now do Exercise 2 on page 41b and Exercise 3 on page 41c.

Professor _____ **Chapter 7/Exercise 1**

Name _____ **Date** _____

Fill in each blank with one of the following words or phrases. Use correct capitalization.

later   finally   during   first   when I arrived

My first day of college was the tensest and most exciting day of my life. I woke up that morning feeling very excited. _____ , I drove to school. It's about five miles. I arrived at school almost a half hour early. _____ , I talked with my friends about our classes. I have two best friends, and we're taking writing, grammar, and speech classes together. _____ , we went into our writing class. _____ the writing class, we were asked to write a paragraph. I was really nervous because I wanted to do a good job on my first assignment. _____ , our teacher asked us to fill out an information page which included our names, where we are from, how many hours we were working per week, which classes we were taking, and many other questions. In brief, the first day of college made me excited and nervous.

Score _____

Professor _____   **Chapter 7/Exercise 2**

Name _____   **Date** _____

Number the following sentences in a logical order.

_____   a. Before you leave, it is a good idea to ask someone to watch your house and take your mail inside.

_____   b. For example, if you are traveling to London, you will want to have warm clothes, whereas if you are going to Hawaii, you will want to pack light clothing.

_____   c. It is easy to plan for a trip abroad if you follow these simple steps.

_____   d. To illustrate, you will want to decide what time of day you want to leave and what price you are willing to pay for an airline ticket.

_____   e. The final step is to leave a copy of your itinerary with a friend at home in case something happens and your family needs to contact you.

_____   f. In conclusion, preparing for a trip overseas is easy.

_____   g. Next, you will want to make sure that your passport is current.

_____   h. You will also want to investigate what the weather is like so you can pack the appropriate clothes.

_____   i. The first step is to check flight times and prices for your trip.

Score _____

Professor _____   **Chapter 7/Exercise 3**

Name _____   **Date** _____

Timed Writing Assignment

Write a process/narrative paragraph on one of the following topics. Skip lines when you write.

Discuss:

Topic A: how to register for classes at your college.
Topic B: the procedure to follow when applying for a job.
Topic C: your most embarrassing moment.
Topic D: the easiest way to wash a dog.
Topic E: how you felt on your first day of school.
Topic F: how to play a particular sport.
Topic G: a special day you spent with your friends or family recently

_____

_____

_____

_____

_____

_____

_____

_____

_____

_____

_____

_____

_____

Score _____

Chapter 8

The Classification Paragraph

In this chapter, you will:
- learn how to write and analyze classification paragraphs.

At the end of the chapter, you will:
- practice writing topic sentences;
- practice using transition words and phrases correctly;
- practice writing support sentences;
- practice analyzing and correcting a classification paragraph; and
- complete a timed writing assignment for a classification paragraph.

This is Elizabeth Dabkowska. You will read her paragraph on pages 45 and 46.

We use the classification paragraph to reflect our tendency to group people, places, and things into various categories. It is human nature. For example, when you meet new students on the first day of class, what is the first thing that you do? Automatically, you look at their appearance, listen to their accents, and try to find out what they do for a living. At that point, you divide the students into groups. One way that people can be classified is by their nationalities (Mexican, Haitian, Japanese, etc.). Another way people can be categorized is by how they dress. Places and things can also be classified.

The Topic Sentence

The topic sentence for the classification paragraph is similar to the topic sentence for the illustration paragraph, but it is acceptable to use only two ideas because classification often requires the use of opposites. However, it is also acceptable to use three, four, or even five ideas in the topic sentence of a classification paragraph.

> • **Examples** •
> a. Teachers can be classified as those who are strict and those who are lenient.
> b. Holidays can be categorized as religious holidays and government holidays.
> c. Animals can be grouped as wild and domestic.

   Now do Exercise 1 on page 47a.

Transition Words and Phrases

There are certain transition words and phrases that are common to the classification paragraph.

> • **Examples** •
> a. ***The first category*** of movies is the action movie.
> b. ***Another way*** that dogs can be classified is by their size.
> c. ***The fourth classification*** of books is the biography.

     d. ***Thirdly***, plants can be categorized as houseplants.

     e. ***The second type*** of phone is the cellular phone.

 Now do Exercise 2 on page 47b and Exercise 3 on page 47c.

The Conclusion Sentence

The conclusion sentence for the classification paragraph is the same as for other types of paragraphs. The transition words and phrases are also similar. The conclusion sentence for this type of paragraph can be general or specific.

    • Examples •

     a. ***In brief***, the Chinese restaurants in Springfield can be categorized as Szechuan, Mandarin, or Cantonese.

     b. ***In summary***, courses at Mason College can be classified as credit and noncredit courses.

Look at the authentic student sample paragraph. Remember that this is a first draft. You will also see the numbers showing errors.

Elizabeth Dabkowska

Schools

What is school like in Poland? How much <u>different</u> <u>there is</u> between Polish and American
                         13   11

schools? Polish <u>student</u> are usually the same age. The biggest <u>differents</u> between them is
          1   18

<u>a</u> way they look. Some kids are shorter or taller. <u>Others are skinnier others are bigger.</u>
          3   9

Of course, there <u>is</u> also very good, <u>intelligence</u> students and students who are not as good
           1   6

and who don't care about their education. Students who are Polish, American, Mexican,

or any other <u>nation</u> are mostly the same. Each country has the same kinds of problems,
6

and each school has similar problems. Students have similar <u>hobby's</u>. They may be more
6

or less intelligent, and they may have more or less difficulty studying or completing

homework, but all of us are the same. _ <u>Didn't</u> matter if your hair is red or blond or
21   4

you are short or tall. <u>All of us are equal, we should all be treated the same.</u>
10

Discussion Questions

1. Does Elizabeth follow the topic? Explain your answer.

   _____

   _____

2. List two ways that Elizabeth can improve her writing for her next assignment.

   a. _____

   b. _____

3. Find the problems with word form in Elizabeth's paragraph and write them correctly.

   a. _____

   b. _____

   c. _____

4. What other grouping of schools is possible?

_____

5. How would you rewrite Elizabeth's conclusion sentence?

_____

_____

➡️ Now do Exercise 4 on page 47d and Exercise 5 on page 47e.

Professor _____   **Chapter 8/Exercise 1**

Name _____   **Date** _____

Use two or three ideas from each of the following brainstorming activities to write a topic sentence for it. Make sure that it is a topic sentence for the classification paragraph.

1.

homework

quizzes

tests

handouts

exercises

exams

group work

_____

2.

Italian food

Mexican food

Brazilian food

expensive food

cheap food

fast food

Chinese food

hot food

cold food

_____

Score _____

Professor _____   **Chapter 8/Exercise 2**

Name _____   **Date** _____

Fill in each blank with a transition word or phrase from this chapter. Use correct punctuation.

Most books can be classified into two groups: fiction and nonfiction.

_____ _____ is fiction. To elaborate, fiction is a

type of writing that is not based in truth. The story is fabricated by the

author. Some examples of fiction are books by Anne Rice, John Grisham,

and Edgar Allan Poe. _____ _____ .

_____ nonfiction is writing that the author says is

factual. It is not a story that is made up by the author. Furthermore, the

author researches, analyzes, and writes what he or she claims to be true.

_____ books can be categorized as fiction and

nonfiction.

Score _____

Pofessor_____   **Chapter 8/Exercise 3**

Name _____   **Date** _____

Write a complete minor support sentence for each of the following major support sentences. Use correct punctuation and appropriate transition words and phrases.

1. One type of phone is the cordless phone.

   _____

2. Another way to classify people is by their religion.

   _____

3. The last way to categorize teachers is by how strict they are.

   _____

4. Secondly, plants can be classified as indoor plants.

   _____

5. Another type of beverage is alcoholic.

   _____

6. The first type of ocean mammal is the whale.

   _____

Score _____

Professor _____   **Chapter 8/Exercise 4**

Name _____   **Date** _____

Rewrite Elizabeth's paragraph on pages 45 and 46. Skip lines when you write.

_____

_____

_____

_____

_____

_____

_____

_____

_____

_____

_____

_____

_____

_____

_____

_____

_____

_____

_____

_____

_____

Score _____

Professor _____   **Chapter 8/Exercise 5**

Name _____   **Date** _____

Timed Writing Assignment

Write a classification paragraph on one of the following topics. Skip lines when you write.

Topic A: Group types of children.
Topic B: Classify types of homes.
Topic C: Discuss the different kinds of attractions found in your city.
Topic D: Explain the different types of computers.
Topic E: Discuss the ways that homes can be classified.
Topic F: Classify some of the kinds of shows on television.

_____

_____

_____

_____

_____

_____

_____

_____

_____

_____

_____

_____

_____

_____

_____

Score _____

Chapter 9

The Descriptive Paragraph

In this chapter, you will:
- learn how to write and analyze descriptive paragraphs.

At the end of this chapter, you will:
- practice using descriptive adjectives;
- practice making general statements more specific;
- practice brainstorming for a descriptive paragraph;
- practice analyzing and correcting a descriptive paragraph; and
- complete a timed writing assignment for a descriptive paragraph.

This is Syed Shahabuddin. You will read his paragraph on pages 51 and 52.

> Writing a descriptive paragraph is like drawing a picture for your readers. Readers should be able to close their eyes and feel as if they have stepped into your paragraph. The descriptive paragraph demonstrates how something looks, feels, tastes, smells, and/or sounds.

The Topic Sentence

There are many ways to write a topic sentence for the descriptive paragraph. Some of the most common ways are by using modifiers (for example, adjectives or adverbs) that will give the reader an overall sense of your description, connecting the sentence to a past experience, and making a statement.

• Examples •

a. The subway stations in Paris are attractive, user friendly, and immaculately clean.   *(modifiers)*
b. My vacation in South Beach last summer was memorable for several reasons.   *(past experience)*
c. The Hudson River is one of the most polluted rivers in the United States. *(fact)*

Transition Words and Phrases

Depending on the type of description, the descriptive paragraph contains a variety of transition words and phrases. For example, a paragraph using the topic sentence in example **a** will usually contain words and phrases for spatial order (for example, *in, on, in front of, next to, to the left of,* and *behind*).

However, a paragraph with a topic sentence similar to example **b** will usually contain general transition words and phrases such as *however, in addition,* and *also.*

Finally, a paragraph using a topic sentence similar to example **c** will usually contain transition words and phrases similar to those used to describe spatial order, but the transitions are usually more specific (for example, *the river bank, the trees,* and *the park*).

• Examples •

a. There are beautiful posters hanging on the clean beige walls of the subway stations.

b. I also enjoyed walking down Ocean Drive, looking at the fabulous cars and trendy restaurants.

c. The river bank in some areas is like a large dumping ground, littered with old tires, aluminum cans, and even abandoned cars.

 Now do Exercise 1 on page 53a, Exercise 2 on page 53b, and Exercise 3 on page 53c.

The Conclusion Sentence

The conclusion sentence for this type of paragraph is similar to the conclusion sentence for other types of paragraphs. However, another transition phrase that can be used to introduce the conclusion sentence for the descriptive paragraph is *Clearly.* This connector demonstrates that you are summarizing and have completed your paragraph.

• Examples •

a. In summary, Paris's subway stations are visually appealing, easy to navigate, and well-maintained.

b. In brief, I'll always remember South Beach as an exciting and enjoyable vacation spot.

c. Clearly, the problem of pollution in the Hudson River needs to be addressed.

Look at the authentic student sample paragraph. Remember that this is a first draft. You will also see the numbers showing errors.

Syed Shahabuddin

My Favorite City

My favorite city is Chittagong. First of all, I was born <u>of</u>

12
this city. There are 300,000 people <u>lived</u> in this wonderful city.

5
Furthermore, it is __ most <u>natural</u> beautiful city in the world. For

21   6
example, there are many hills and trees around the whole city.

Secondly, there is an area near the city, it is called Bay of Bengal.
                                                                    10
It makes it more beautiful than other <u>city</u>. Chittagong has many
                                      2
historical places. For example, the king's palace is in this <u>City</u>, and
                                                              19
many tourists come to visit its marvelous monuments. In conclusion,

Chittagong is the most beautiful city in the world.

Discussion Questions

1. List two positive aspects of Syed's paragraph.

    a. _____

    _____

    b. _____

    _____

2. List two ways that Syed can improve his writing for his next assignment.

    a. _____

    _____

    b. _____

    _____

3. List four of the most powerful modifiers in Syed's paragraph.

   a. _____

   b. _____

   c. _____

   d. _____

➡ Now do Exercise 4 on page 53d and Exercise 5 on page 53e.

Professor _____   **Chapter 9/Exercise 1**

Name _____   **Date** _____

Fill in each blank with an appropriate adjective.

My _____ Italian restaurant was really _____

on Saturday night. Every table was _____ . _____

waiters were running around pouring _____ wine, yelling to

the cooks to hurry up with the orders. You could smell the aroma of

_____ pasta dishes and _____ bread the moment

you walked in. A group of _____ musicians circled the

restaurant, playing _____ songs. When they brought out my

dinner, my mouth began to water. My lasagna was _____ and

_____ . The candles on my table were _____ for

my romantic evening. Clearly, my favorite Italian restaurant was extremely

busy on Saturday night.

Score _____

Professor _____   **Chapter 9/Exercise 2**

Name _____   **Date** _____

Add details to each of the following general statements to make each one more specific.

1. The park is pretty in the springtime.

   _____

2. My niece is a tall girl.

   _____

3. Her closet is a mess.

   _____

4. Colorado is a beautiful place to visit when it snows.

   _____

5. Robert's car is sporty.

   _____

6. The new Italian restaurant was busy on Saturday night.

   _____

7. The Christmas concert was wonderful.

   _____

8. Cell phones are very popular in the United States.

   _____

Score _____

Professor _____   **Chapter 9/Exercise 3**

Name _____   **Date** _____

Look around your classroom. What do you see? Do a brainstorming activity to describe your classroom. Use words and phrases that describe spatial order. Write a topic sentence, using the brainstorming ideas.

Brainstorming Ideas

_____   _____   _____

_____   _____   _____

_____   _____   _____

Topic Sentence

_____

Score _____

Professor _____   **Chapter 9/Exercise 4**

Name _____   **Date** _____

Rewrite Syed's paragraph on pages 51 and 52. Skip lines when you write.

_____

_____

_____

_____

_____

_____

_____

_____

_____

_____

_____

_____

_____

_____

_____

_____

_____

_____

_____

_____

_____

_____

_____

Score _____

Professor _____   **Chapter 9/Exercise 5**

Name _____   **Date _____**

Timed Writing Assignment

Write a descriptive paragraph on one of the following topics. Skip lines when you write.

Topic A: Describe one of your classmates.
Topic B: Describe your favorite restaurant.
Topic C: Describe the room in your house where you spend the most time.
Topic D: Describe the most interesting landmark in your hometown.
Topic E: Describe a close friend or family member.

Score _____

Chapter 10

The Definition Paragraph

In this chapter, you will:
- learn how to write and analyze definition paragraphs.

At the end of the chapter, you will:
- practice using transition words and phrases correctly;
- practice matching major support with minor support for a definition paragraph;
- practice writing topic sentences for a definition paragraph;
- practice analyzing and correcting a definition paragraph; and
- complete a timed writing assignment for a definition paragraph.

This is Andrea Barrigan. Is the man with Andrea her perfect man? You will read her paragraph on page 58.

A definition paragraph not only defines something, but distinguishes it from similar items. For example, if an assignment requires a definition of the word *computer*, you have to decide how to distinguish it from other types of machines. You know that computers can calculate, analyze, store, and process data more efficiently than other machines. With this information in mind, you can write a correct topic sentence.

The Topic Sentence

The topic sentence for this type of paragraph is different from topic sentences for other types of paragraphs. It has two parts. The first part of the topic sentence contains what is being defined and a word that indicates its general category. The second part contains a relative pronoun and three or more distinguishing characteristics. (See Chapter 3 for a list of relative pronouns.)

In each of the following sentences, the item being defined is underlined, its general category is in boldface type, and the distinguishing features are in italic type.

> • **Examples** •
>
> a. <u>The perfect friend</u> can be defined as **a person** who is *trustworthy*, *caring*, and *fun to be with*.
>
> b. <u>Jealousy</u> can be defined as **an emotion** which makes you feel *insecure*, *angry*, and *hateful*.
>
> c. <u>The Fourth of July</u> can be defined as **a holiday** when Americans *celebrate their independence*, *have barbecues*, and *watch fireworks*.

In example **a**, the writer is defining the perfect friend. A perfect friend can be put into the general category of people, but what makes the perfect friend different from other people is that he or she is trustworthy, caring, and fun to be with.

Similarly, an item is defined, categorized, and explained in example **b** and in example **c**.

 Now do Exercise 1 on page 59a.

Transition Words and Phrases

Some transition words and phrases are usually used only in the definition paragraph, but many of those used in the classification paragraph can also be used.

- **Examples** •
    a. ***The first way to define*** the perfect friend is that he or she is a trustworthy companion.

    b. ***The second characteristic*** of jealousy is that it makes you feel insecure about yourself.

    c. Finally, the Fourth of July can be ***differentiated from*** other holidays because people usually watch fireworks.

 Now do Exercise 2 on page 59b.

The Conclusion Sentence

The conclusion sentence for the definition paragraph is the same as with most of the other types of paragraphs. The conclusion sentence can be either specific (using synonyms) or general.

- **Examples** •

    General

    a. In brief, the perfect friend should have these three characteristics.

    Specific

    b. In conclusion, being jealous makes you feel bad about yourself, makes you get angry easily, and causes you to be mean to other people.

 Now do Exercise 3 on page 59c.

Look at the authentic student paragraph on the next page. Remember that this is a first draft. You will also see the numbers showing errors.

Andrea Barragan

The Perfect Man

The perfect man has to have the Brad Pitt's blond hair, his blue eyes, and his square face. Nicholas Cage's full lips. I would like an athletic body like David Hasselhoff's body and big hands and long finger like _ famous Pianist Rachmaninov. He should have strong arms like Sylvester Stallone. His muscles, too. I prefer long, strong legs. In conclusion, I want an impossible man.

Discussion Questions

1. List two positive aspects of Andrea's paragraph.

a. _____

_____

b. _____

_____

2. List two ways that Andrea can improve her writing for her next assignment.

a. _____

_____

b. _____

_____

3. List and correct the fragments in Andrea's paragraph.

a. _____

_____

b. _____

_____

➡️ Now do Exercise 4 on page 59d and Exercise 5 on page 59e.

Professor _____   **Chapter 10/Exercise 1**

Name _____   **Date** _____

Brainstorm and write a topic sentence for each of the following topics.

Topic A: Define love.

_____   _____   _____

_____   _____   _____

Topic Sentence

_____

_____

Topic B: Define freedom.

_____   _____   _____

_____   _____   _____

Topic Sentence

_____

_____

Topic C: Define a good parent.

_____   _____   _____

_____   _____   _____

Topic Sentence

_____

_____

Topic D: Define a successful student.

_____   _____   _____

_____   _____   _____

Topic Sentence

_____

_____

Score _____

Professor _____   **Chapter 10/Exercise 2**

Name _____   **Date** _____

Fill in each blank with a transition word or phrase from this chapter. Use correct punctuation.

A typical teenager is a person who rebels against his or her parents,

_____ , and _____ . The first way

to define a teenager is as a person who rebels against his or her parents.

For example, some teenagers break their parents' rules, such as having to

be home by a certain time at night. Typical teenagers can also be differ-

entiated from other people because they _____

_____ . To illustrate, _____

_____ . The final _____ of a typical

teenager is _____ . To

demonstrate, _____

_____ . In conclusion, _____

_____ .

Score _____

Professor _____   **Chapter 10/Exercise 3**

Name _____   **Date** _____

Match the major support on the left with the best possible minor support on the right. Use each only once.

1. A good friend also keeps your secrets.

2. Another way autobiographies can be differentiated from other types of books is that they are written by the principal character.

3. Horses can also be defined according to their ability to carry a rider.

4. The second characteristic of a good baby is that he or she doesn't cry often.

5. The first characteristic of the cellular phone is its cordless mechanism.

6. The final way to define a good teacher is by the methods that he or she uses.

a. To elaborate, he or she sleeps, plays, and cuddles most of the time.

b. To illustrate, you don't need to stand next to the base to talk to someone.

c. For example, he or she uses lectures, group work, and individual study.

d. To demonstrate, my friend Susan never repeats to others what I tell her.

e. For example, Frank Sinatra wrote a book about himself called *My Way*.

f. To illustrate, a dog or cat cannot hold a person on its back.

Score _____

Professor _____   **Chapter 10/Exercise 4**

Name _____   **Date** _____

Rewrite Andrea's paragraph on page 58. Skip lines when you write.

_____

_____

_____

_____

_____

_____

_____

_____

_____

_____

_____

_____

_____

_____

_____

_____

_____

_____

_____

Score _____

Professor _____   **Chapter 10/Exercise 5**

Name _____   **Date** _____

Timed Writing Assignment

Write a definition paragraph on one of the following topics. Skip lines when you write.

Topic A: What are some characteristics of a good boss?
Topic B: What is happiness to you or someone you know?
Topic C: What are some of the attributes of your favorite car?
Topic D: What makes a great vacation for you?
Topic E: What is a family?

_____

_____

_____

_____

_____

_____

_____

_____

_____

_____

_____

_____

_____

_____

_____

Score _____

Chapter 11

The Comparison Paragraph

In this chapter, you will:
- learn how to write and analyze comparison paragraphs.

At the end of the chapter, you will:
- practice writing topic sentences;
- practice writing conclusion sentences;
- practice analyzing and correcting a comparison paragraph; and
- complete a timed writing assignment for a comparison paragraph.

This is Denise Francois. You will read her paragraph on page 63.

We use the comparison paragraph to show how two or more people or things are similar to each other. This type of paragraph uses vivid examples to demonstrate the similarity in characteristics.

The Topic Sentence

The topic sentence for the comparison paragraph must be specific. It should contain the main points of your paragraph, and it should be the first sentence of your paragraph.

> • **Examples** •
>
> a. Pepsi and Coca-Cola are similar because both contain caffeine, have more than ninety calories per serving, and are carbonated.
>
> b. Grammar class and reading class have similar characteristics, such as exams, required class participation, and homework.
>
> c. Vacations at the beach and in the mountains are alike in their high cost, relaxing atmosphere, and beautiful scenery

Notice that in examples **a**, **b**, **d**, and **e**, there is a comma after the transition word or phrase, followed by an independent clause. There is no comma in example **c**.

 Now do Exercise 1 on page 63a.

Transition Words and Phrases

Some transition words and phrases are common to the comparison paragraph.

> • **Examples** •
>
> a. *Each* of my friends is trustworthy.
> b. *Both* dogs *and* cats make good pets.
> c. *Neither* Joe's Steakhouse *nor* China Moon serves breakfast.
> d. You can use *either* the Macintosh *or* the PC for spreadsheets.
> e. My mother and father are *alike* in their religious beliefs.
> f. My niece, *like* my nephew, is a good athlete.
> g. Cancún is *similar to* the Bahamas because of its exquisite white sandy beaches.
> i. *In the same way* that babies need lots of attention, *so* do puppies.
> j. Teachers *as well as* students have to study.
> k. My little sister *also* likes to show her independence.

Look at the authentic student sample paragraph.

Denise Francois

Similarities Between My Mother and Me

My mother and I are similar in many <u>way</u>. <u>For example, our bodies.</u>
2   8
If you look <u>to</u> my <u>mother</u> body and my body, there are no differences at
12   6
all. We wear the same size clothes and shoes. We _ also alike in our taste
21
<u>for</u> food, people, and clothes. In the same way that my mother <u>like</u> to
12   1
be helpful, so do I. <u>She loves to be with her kids, I do too.</u> My mother
10
and I <u>we</u> are very similar. Sometimes we even dream the same things.
21

Discussion Questions

1. List two positive aspects of Denise's paragraph.

   a. _____

   b. _____

2. List two ways that Denise can improve her writing for her next assignment.

   a. _____

   b. _____

3. How could this comparison be written more effectively?

   _____

4. How would you rewrite Denise's conclusion sentence?

   _____

 Now do Exercise 2 on page 63b, Exercise 3 on page 63c, and Exercise 4 on page 63d.

Professor _____ **Chapter 11/Exercise 1**

Name _____ **Date** _____

Write a topic sentence comparing each of the following.

1. two friends

_____

_____

2. two cities

_____

_____

3. English and your first language

_____

_____

4. two books

_____

_____

5. two restaurants

_____

_____

Score _____

Professor _____　　　**Chapter 11/Exercise 2**

Name _____　　　**Date** _____

Write conclusion sentences, using your topic sentences from Exercise 1.

1. _____

   _____

2. _____

   _____

3. _____

   _____

4. _____

   _____

5. _____

   _____

Score _____

Professor _____   **Chapter 11/Exercise 3**

Name _____   **Date** _____

Rewrite Denise's paragraph on page 63. Skip write.

_____

_____

_____

_____

_____

_____

_____

_____

_____

_____

_____

_____

_____

_____

_____

_____

_____

_____

_____

_____

_____

_____

Score _____

Professor _____   **Chapter 11/Exercise 4**

Name _____   **Date** _____

Timed Writing Assignment

Write a comparison paragraph on one of the following topics. Skip lines when you write.

Topic A: two of your teachers (for example, *your English teacher*).
Topic B: two types of cars (for example, *Pontiac Grand Am*).
Topic C: two sit-down restaurants (for example, *Red Lobster*).
Topic D: two of your relatives (for example, *your cousin*).
Topic E: two holidays (for example, *New Year's Eve*).
Topic F: two types of technology (for example, *cellular phones*).

_____

_____

_____

_____

_____

_____

_____

_____

_____

_____

_____

_____

_____

_____

_____

_____

_____

Score _____

Chapter 12

The Contrast Paragraph

In this chapter, you will:
- learn how to write and analyze contrast paragraphs.

At the end of the chapter, you will:
- practice brainstorming for a contrast paragraph;
- practice writing major support sentences for a contrast paragraph;
- practice analyzing and correcting a contrast paragraph; and
- complete a timed writing assignment for a contrast paragraph.

This is Lucny B. Vincent. You will read her paragraph on pages 67 and 68.

We use the contrast paragraph to illustrate how two or more people or things are different from each other. Using colorful and descriptive examples helps to illustrate these differences.

The Topic Sentence

The topic sentence for the contrast paragraph should contain at least three main points. These ideas should be contained in the first sentence of the paragraph.

• Examples •

a. Horses and cows are different because of their physical structure, their uses, and their digestive processes.
b. Miami and New York are dissimilar because of their population densities, the weather, and the ethnic backgrounds of the residents.
c. Fast-food and full-service restaurants differ in their prices, service, and atmosphere.

Transition Words and Phrases

Some transition words and phrases are common to the contrast paragraph.

• Examples •

a. The second way that children and teenagers are **not similar** is in their experience.
b. **Unlike** dogs, cats hate water.
c. Parents love their children **differently** from the way that they love each other.
d. Solar power and electric power are **different** in terms of the cost involved to operate them.
e. They also **differ** because of their commitment.
f. **Dissimilarly**, parents have many responsibilities that couples without children do not have.
g. Black-and-white photography and color photography are **dissimilar** due to the time it takes to process the photos.
h. Men and women are **not alike** in their physical appearance.

 Now do Exercise 1 on page 69a and Exercise 2 on page 69b.

Look at the authentic student sample paragraph. Remember that this is a first draft. You will also see the numbers showing errors.

Lucny B. Vincent

Schools

I am going to tell you about the differences with high
                                                        12
school in Haiti and college in the United States. Some differences

were the time to finish a level, the language, and financial aids.
 4   2
First, in my country, high school students take one year to finish

a level. For example, it took me one year to go from nineth grade
                                                            18
to tenth grade, but in the United States, I can take three

English language levels in one year. For example, Beginning 1 English

in one semester, Beginning 2 English in the second semester, and
                                     8
Intermediate 1 in third semester. This equal one year. Second, when
                                          2
I was in Haiti, I spoke Creole, but my teacher teaches the class
                                                    4
in French. However, in the United States, the teachers speak only

English, and the students in our language program speak many

difference languages, such as Creole, Russian, Thai, _ Spanish.
    6   21
Another big opportunity that students in the United States have
                                                    10
is the financial aid, in Haiti we don't have it at all. In conclusion,

the success of schools depend on the government in all countries.
                              1

Discussion Questions

1. List two positive aspects of Lucny's paragraph.

   a. _____

   _____

   b. _____

   _____

2. List two ways Lucny can improve her writing for her next assignment.

   a. _____

   _____

   b. _____

   _____

3. Does Lucny use effective minor support sentences? _____
   If not, how would you change the minor support?

   _____

   _____

   _____

4. Choose one minor support sentence and give a different example.

   _____

   _____

   _____

➡ Now do Exercise 3 on page 69c and Exercise 4 on page 69d.

Professor _____   **Chapter 12/Exercise 1**

Name _____   **Date** _____

Brainstorm on the following topics.

1. Contrast being old and being young.

   _____   _____   _____

   _____   _____   _____

   _____   _____   _____

2. Contrast economy cars and luxury cars.

   _____   _____   _____

   _____   _____   _____

   _____   _____   _____

3. Contrast having a college education and not having one.

   _____   _____   _____

   _____   _____   _____

   _____   _____   _____

4. Contrast people who have children and those who do not.

   _____   _____   _____

   _____   _____   _____

   _____   _____   _____

Score _____

Professor _____   **Chapter 12/Exercise 2**

Name _____   **Date** _____

Write a major support sentence for each of the following minor support sentences.

1. _____

   For example, dogs like to chase cars, but cats don't.

2. _____

   For example, cats don't have to be walked several times a day.

3. _____

   To demonstrate, people who have pets live longer than people who don't.

4. _____

   To illustrate, rattlesnakes are poisonous, but grass snakes aren't.

5. _____

   This can be proved because people who go to college have a better chance of getting a high-paying job.

6. _____

   To demonstrate, smokers have a higher incidence of lung cancer.

Score _____

Professor _____　　**Chapter 12/Exercise 3**

Name _____　　**Date** _____

Rewrite Lucny's paragraph on pages 67 and 68. Skip lines when you write.

_____

_____

_____

_____

_____

_____

_____

_____

_____

_____

_____

_____

_____

_____

_____

_____

_____

_____

_____

_____

_____

_____

_____

Score _____

Professor _____   **Chapter 12/Exercise 4**

Name _____   **Date** _____

Timed Writing Assignment

Write a contrast paragraph on one of the following topics. Skip lines when you write.

Topic A: Discuss the differences between children with no siblings and children from large families.

Topic B: Contrast two types of pets.

Topic C: Discuss the dissimilarities between being married and being single.

Topic D: Demonstrate the differences between two classes that you have taken within the last year.

Topic E: Contrast two of your friends.

Topic F: Show the differences between your lifestyle now and how you think your lifestyle will be ten years from now.

_____

_____

_____

_____

_____

_____

_____

_____

_____

_____

_____

_____

_____

_____

Score _____

Answer Keys

Chapter 1

Chapter 1/Exercise 1

1. (When John gets home,) he'll make a telephone call.

2. Anton goes to school on Mondays, Wednesdays, and Fridays.

3. (After Marie went swimming,) she was hungry.

4. Erin loves spring, (but she hates summer.)

5. Don't go to sleep (until you call your brother.)

6. The teacher is here.

7. Mr. Baptiste sings and dances.

8. The girls next door are coming to our party.

9. Jim's trying to save money (because he's flying to Switzerland next summer.)

10. Cats are great pets, and they're easy to take care of.

11. Jay's leaving for California on Thursday, and he's returning on Tuesday.

12. Gail threw an anniversary party for her parents.

Chapter 1/Exercise 2

1. C	4. ✓	7. F	10. ✓
2. F	5. C	8. ✓	11. C
3. R	6. F	9. R	12. R

Chapter 1/Exercise 3

Answers may vary.

1. X My bedroom has a large dresser with a mirror.
2. ✓
3. X Robert's band is playing tonight at the Warehouse Café, and all his friends are going there to watch him.
4. X Because she was working on a new project, Louise worked late in her office last night.
5. ✓
6. X Dan and Kate rented a movie last night. It was their favorite.

Chapter 1/Exercise 4

Answers will vary.

Chapter 2

Chapter 2/Exercise 1

1. The students must study for the test, or they will fail it.
2. The lobster smells delicious, and it looks good, too.
3. The Hoffmans don't want to stay home for Christmas, yet/but they don't want to travel far.
4. Carl's in love with Gina, so he's going to ask her to marry him.
5. Maria needs a vacation, for she has been working very hard.
6. Henry doesn't want to go to the movies tonight, but/yet he doesn't want to rent a video.

Chapter 2/Exercise 2

1. CP	4. CX	7. S	10. CP
2. S	5. S	8. CP	11. CX
3. CX	6. CX	9. S	12. CP

Chapter 2/Exercise 3

Answers may vary.

1. Tonight I'll go to your house, <u>or</u> you can come to my house.
2. I always brush my teeth <u>when</u> I wake up in the morning.
   When I wake up in the morning, I always brush my teeth.
3. Sam stayed in Hawaii an extra week <u>because</u> he was having lots of fun.
   Because he was having lots of fun, Sam stayed in Hawaii an extra week.

4. <u>When/While</u> Marty was taking a shower, the phone rang.

   The phone rang when/while Marty was taking a shower.

5. You'll fail the test <u>unless</u> you study very hard this week.

   Unless you study very hard this week, you'll fail the test.

6. I want to eat chicken for dinner, <u>and</u> I want to have cake for dessert.

7. John and his girlfriend will help you <u>because</u> they're your friends.

   Because John and his girlfriend are your friends, they'll help you.

8. Steve didn't wash the dishes, <u>but</u> he swept the floor.

Chapter 2/Exercise 4

Answers will vary. Here are some possibilities.

1. We want to throw a party so that we can celebrate your birthday.

2. When you arrive in France, you'll have to show your ticket and your passport.

3. The dog will be fed by the neighbors because we will be on vacation.

4. She'll wait for you until you get there.

5. If you do all the work, you'll pass the class.

6. You don't have a boyfriend, yet you want to get married.

7. As soon as Christine gets home, we can go to the movies.

8. While you were shopping, the letter carrier came with a package for you.

Chapter 2/Exercise 5

1. Ross, who got a promotion last month, also got a raise.

2. Many scientists are searching for a cure for cancer, which is a common disease.

3. Hank likes to travel with Jill, who is his wife.

4. Robert Browning, whom Elizabeth Barrett married, is a famous poet.

5. Samantha's favorite play is *Hamlet,* which was written by William Shakespeare.

6. Steve, who you met last night, is my older brother.

7. Tony, who is the best student in the class, is from Chile.

8. Chip lives in Spring Valley, which is a small town in Virginia.

9. Tom Hanks, whom we saw on TV last night, is an accomplished actor.

10. The Nile, which is in Africa, is the longest river in the world.

Chapter 2/Exercise 6

Answers will vary.

Chapter 3

Chapter 3/Exercise 1

Answers will vary

Chapter 3/Exercise 2

Answers will vary

Chapter 3/Exercise 3

Answers will vary. Here are some possibilities.

Topic Sentence: Living alone is different from living with others because of expenses, housekeeping chores, and independence.

  I. One of the differences concerns expenses.

    A. You have to pay rent and utility bills by yourself if you live alone.

    B. You have to buy all your own furniture and appliances.

  II. Another contrast is in the housekeeping chores.

    A. You can share chores if you live with others.

    B. More free time to do other things.

  III. The final difference is in independence.

    A. You have more privacy if you live alone.

    B. If you live with others, you have to respect their rules.

Conclusion Sentence: In conclusion, there are many differences between living by yourself and living with other people.

Chapter 3/Exercise 4

Answers will vary.

Chapter 4

Chapter 4/Exercise 1

Answers will vary. Here are some possibilities.

1. The best way to choose a car is to look in car magazines, find information on the Internet, and ask friends for recommendations.
2. It's smart to finish your education because you will get a better job, a higher salary, and personal satisfaction.

3. The perfect spouse is kind, funny, and responsible.
4. My classroom has Peruvian, Colombian, Cuban, and Russian students.
5. Being married and being single are similar because friends, family, and individual growth are important to all people involved.
6. Three differences between being married and single are independence, finances, and free time.
7. I enjoy reading because it relaxes me and allows me to visit new places without leaving my living room.
8. Exercising regularly helps keep you physically healthy and can make you feel better about yourself.

Chapter 4/Exercise 2

1. c   2. b   3. a   4. c

Chapter 4/Exercise 3

Answers may vary.
1. #1: First of all, using public transportation is a good idea because it saves money.
    #2: Second, using public transportation helps the environment.
    #3: The final reason is that it is safer than driving a car.
2. #1: Firstly, adults and children are not alike in their experience.
    #2: Secondly, they are dissimilar in their health status.
    #3: They also differ in their financial situations.

Chapter 4/Exercise 4

Answers will vary. Here are some possibilities.
1. For example, when a spouse finds love outside of marriage, it can lead to divorce.
2. To illustrate, cats don't need to be walked, and you only have to leave some food and water for them.
3. To demonstrate, the college library is quiet and conducive to studying.
4. To elaborate, the perfect friend will keep all your secrets.
5. For example, we napped in the sun and slept late whenever we wanted to.

Chapter 4/Exercise 5

Answers will vary.

Chapter 5

Chapter 5/Exercise 1

Answers may vary.

How to Get an A

I <u>likes</u> to get an A <u>at</u> class, but I need_study every day. <u>I often go to</u>
    1   12   21
<u>the library at night, that is how I prepare for class.</u> I <u>reads</u> the newspaper
        10   1
every day. <u>And grammar books before I go to sleep.</u> I <u>Listen</u> to the radio or
                            8   19
watch TV daily. I <u>am speaking</u> English with my friends in work and on bus.
                 4

How to Get an A
I would like to get an A in class, but I need to study every day. I often go to the library at night, and that is how I prepare for class. I read the newspaper every day and grammar books before I go to sleep. I listen to the radio or watch TV daily. I speak English with my friends at work and on the bus. In conclusion, if I follow these steps, I can get an A in class.

Chapter 6

Chapter 6/Discussion Questions

Answers may vary.
1. Yes, it is. There are three main points in the topic sentence.
2. a. She should check punctuation.
   b. She should check singular/plural usage.
3. Yes, it includes very detailed examples.
4. Yes, it is very similar to the topic sentence.

Chapter 6/Exercise 1

Answers may vary.

Miami is a great place for vacation because of the attractions, the beaches, and the weather. <u>The first reason</u> Miami is a good vacation spot is the attractions. <u>To illustrate,</u> Miami has the Seaquarium, Vizcaya, and Bayside Marketplace. <u>Secondly,</u> Miami is a good vacation spot because of the beaches. <u>For example,</u> Miami has white sand, blue water, and beautiful palm trees. <u>The final reason</u> this vacation spot is wonderful is the weather. <u>To demonstrate,</u> the temperature is rarely under 70 degrees, and it's usually sunny. <u>In brief,</u> Miami is a fantastic spot for vacation.

Chapter 6/Exercise 2

Answers will vary.

1. The second reason that a college education is important <u>is the prestige.</u>

2. For example<u>, they clean themselves and do not need to be bathed.</u>

3. Watching movies is a good way to learn English because you can hear correct pronunciation, learn new vocabulary, and talk about the movie with your friends. First<u>, you can hear correct pronunciation.</u>

4. It's difficult to attend school while working because you don't have time to study. To illustrate<u>, you might have only one hour each night to spend on homework.</u>

Chapter 6/Exercise 3

Answers will vary.

      Incompatibility, infidelity, and drug or alcohol problems are some of the most common reasons that there is an increase in the number of people who get divorced. First of all, incompatibility is a reason for divorce. For example, people who have an unrealistic view of married life will soon be disappointed when they realize that to be married means not only to have romantic love, but also to have family obligations. Also, infidelity can poison family life. For instance, if the spouses don't have areas of shared contentment and do not unite with common ideas of life, they will try to find all that is necessary for the soul and the body with another person. Drug and alcohol problems are common factors in life and have destructive roles. To illustrate, nobody wants to be the target of love for the person who has immoral habits. In conclusion, problems such as incompatibility, infidelity, and drug or alcohol abuse can be the cause of divorce.

Chapter 6/Exercise 4

Answers will vary.

Chapter 7 _____

Chapter 7/Discussion Questions (Paragraph #1)

Answers may vary.

1. Yes
   a. First of all   b. For example   c. Finally
2. a. It includes good details.
   b. It includes good use of transition words and phrases.
3. a. He should be clear regarding the type of paragraph.
   b. He should check for omitted words.

Chapter 7/Discussion Questions (Paragraph #2)

Answers may vary.

1. Second, I have better educational opportunities. I did not have them in my country.
2. In conclusion, my arrival in the United States was the happiest day in my life for several reasons.
3. a. She shows a lot of emotion in her writing.

   b. She uses vivid examples.
4. a. She should check verb tense.

   b. She should check for omitted words.

Chapter 7/Exercise 1

My first day of college was the tensest and most exciting day of my life. <u>First</u>, I drove to school. It's about five miles. I arrived at school almost a half hour early. <u>When I arrived</u>, I talked with my friends about our classes. I have two best friends, and we're taking writing, grammar, and speech classes together. <u>Later</u>, we went into our writing class. <u>During</u> the writing class, we were asked to write a paragraph. I was really nervous because I wanted to do a good job on my first assignment. <u>Finally</u>, our teacher asked us to fill out an information page which included our names, where we are from, how many hours we were working per week, which classes we were taking, and many other questions. In brief, the first day of college made me excited and nervous.

Chapter 7/Exercise 2

Answers may vary.

The likely order of the sentences is: c, i, d, g, h, b, a, e, f.

Chapter 7/Exercise 3

Answers will vary.

Chapter 8

Chapter 8 Discussion Questions

Answers may vary.

1. No, there isn't a clear topic sentence.
2. a. She should state a topic sentence and follow it more closely.

   b. She should check sentence structure, such as run-on sentences and comma splices.

   3. a. intelligent; intelligence
      b. nation; nationality
      c. hobby's; hobbies
   4. private and public schools
   5. In conclusion, schools can be classified as Polish and American.

Chapter 8/Exercise 1

Answers will vary. Here are some possibilities.

   1. Teachers use several tools to assess students' progress, such as homework, quizzes, and exams.
   2. Three of the most popular types of food in the United States are Italian, Chinese, and Mexican.

Chapter 8/Exercise 2

Answers may vary.

   Most books can be classified into two groups: fiction and nonfiction. <u>The first type of book</u> is fiction. To elaborate, fiction is a type of writing that is not based in truth. The story is fabricated by the author. Some examples of fiction are books by Anne Rice, John Grisham, and Edgar Allen Poe. <u>The second type is nonfiction</u>. <u>To elaborate,</u> nonfiction is writing that the author says is factual. It is not a story that is made up by the author. Furthermore, the author researches, analyzes, and writes what he or she claims to be true. <u>In brief,</u> books can be categorized as fiction and nonfiction.

Chapter 8/Exercise 3

Answers will vary. Here are some possibilities.

   1. For example, you can carry this phone all around the house and even outdoors.
   2. To illustrate, people can be Catholic, Jewish, Buddhist, or any of several other different religions.
   3. To demonstrate, strict teachers expect students to be quiet, speak only when they are called on, and complete all their assignments on time.
   4. Some types of indoor plants are herbs, palms, and cactus plants.
   5. Some alcoholic beverages are rum, vodka, and bourbon.
   6. To elaborate, whales are beautiful creatures that feed on the ocean plants and animals, and their young are born alive.

Chapter 8/Exercise 4

Answers may vary.

Two types of schools are Polish and American. How much difference is there between Polish and American schools? Polish students are usually the same age. The biggest difference between them is the way they look. Some kids are shorter or taller. Others are skinnier, and others are bigger. Of course, there are also very good, intelligent students, and students who are not as good and who don't care about their education. Students who are Polish, American, Mexican, or any other nationality are mostly the same. Each country has the same kinds of problems, and each school has similar problems. Students have similar hobbies. They may be more or less intelligent, and they may have more or less difficulty studying or completing homework, but all of us are the same. It doesn't matter if your hair is red or blond or you are short or tall. In conclusion, schools can be classified as Polish and American.

Chapter 8/Exercise 5

Answers will vary.

Chapter 9

Chapter 9 Discussion Questions

Answers may vary.

1. a. It includes good, specific details (for example, "300,000 people").
    b. It includes a good conclusion sentence.
2. a. His topic sentence should be more detailed.
    b. He should check for comma splices.
3. a. wonderful
    b. beautiful
    c. historical
    d. marvelous

Chapter 9/Exercise 1

Answers may vary.

My <u>favorite</u> Italian restaurant was really <u>busy</u> on Saturday night. Every table was <u>occupied</u>. <u>Frenzied</u> waiters were running around pouring <u>fine</u> wine, yelling to the cooks to hurry up with the orders. You could smell the aroma of <u>delicious</u> pasta dishes and <u>fresh</u> bread the moment you walked in. A group of cheerful musicians circled the restaurant, playing <u>romantic</u> songs. When they brought out my dinner, my mouth began to water. My lasagna was <u>hot</u> and <u>tasty</u>. The candles on my table were <u>perfect</u> for my romantic evening. Clearly, my favorite restaurant was extremely busy on Saturday night.

Chapter 9/Exercise 2

Answers will vary. Here are some possibilities.

1. Because of the beautiful wildflowers, the park is pretty in the springtime.
2. My niece is 6 feet 3 inches tall.
3. Her closet is a mess, for she has clothes on the floor and her shoes are everywhere.
4. Colorado is a beautiful place to visit when it snows because all the buildings and streets are covered in a clean white blanket.
5. Robert's car is a sporty red Corvette.
6. The new Italian restaurant was so busy on Saturday night that we had to wait an hour for a table.
7. Because of the children's choir and the inspirational music, the Christmas concert was wonderful.
8. In 1997, more than 55 million cell phones were in use in the United States.

Chapter 9/Exercise 3

Answers will vary.

Chapter 9/Exercise 4

My Favorite City

My favorite city is Chittagong. First of all, I was born in this city. There are 300,000 people living in this wonderful city. Furthermore, it is the most naturally beautiful city in the world. For example, there are many hills and trees around the whole city. Secondly, there is an area near the city that it is called the Bay of Bengal. It makes it more beautiful than other cities. Chittagong has many historical places. For example, the king's palace is in this city, and many tourists come to visit its marvelous monuments. In conclusion, Chittagong is the most beautiful city in the world.

Chapter 9/Exercise 5

Answers will vary.

Chapter 10

Chapter 10 Discussion Questions

Answers may vary.

1. a. It includes several examples.
   b. It includes vivid details.
2. a. She should check for fragments.
   b. She should check for omitted or unnecessary words and phrases.
3. a. Nicholas Cage's full lips.; He should have Nicholas Cage's full lips.
   b. His muscles, too.; He should have his muscles, too.

Chapter 10/Exercise 1

Answers will vary.

Chapter 10/Exercise 2

Answers will vary.

A typical teenager is a person who rebels against his or her parents, dresses in the current style, and spends a lot of time with friends. The first way to define a teenager is as a person who rebels against his or her parents. For example, some teenagers break their parents' rules, such as having to be home by a certain time at night. Typical teenagers can also be differentiated from other people because they dress in the current style. To illustrate, teenagers these days wear very baggy pants and large necklaces. The final characteristic of a typical teenager is that he or she spends a lot of time with friends. To demonstrate, my cousin spends several hours each day with his friends. In conclusion, a typical teenager is rebellious, trendy, and social.

Chapter 10/Exercise 3

1. d	3. f	5. b
2. e	4. a	6. c

Chapter 10/Exercise 4

Answers may vary.

The perfect man has to have Brad Pitt's blond hair, his blue eyes, and his square face. He should have Nicholas Cage's full lips. I would like an athletic body like David Hasselhoff's body and big hands and long fingers like the famous pianist Rachmaninov. He should have strong arms and muscles like Sylvester Stallone. He should have his muscles, too. I prefer long, strong legs. In conclusion, I want an impossible man.

Chapter 10/Exercise 5

Answers will vary.

Chapter 11 _____

Chapter 11 Discussion Questions

Answers may vary.

1. a. It includes good main points.
   b. It includes vivid details.
2. a. She should check preposition use.
   b. She should check sentence structure (for example, fragments and comma splices).

3. She could give examples of food, people, and clothes.

4. In brief, my mother and I are so similar that we sometimes even dream the same things.

Chapter 11/Exercise 1
Answers will vary.

Chapter 11/Exercise 2
Answers will vary.

Chapter 11/Exercise 3
Answers will vary.

My mother and I are similar in many ways. For example, our bodies are alike. If you look at my mother's body and my body, there are no differences at all. We wear the same size clothes and shoes. We are also alike in our taste in food, people, and clothes. In the same way that my mother likes to be helpful, so do I. She loves to be with her kids, and I do too. In brief, my mother and I are so similar that we sometimes even dream the same things.

Chapter 12

Chapter 12 Discussion Questions
Answers may vary.

1. a. The ideas follow the topic sentence.

   b. It includes support for most of the ideas.

2. a. She should check verb tense.

   b. She should check sentence structure (for example, fragments and comma splices).

3. No.

   She could include more details, such as a better explanation of financial aid in the U.S.

4. For example, teachers in the United States speak only English during the class, at meetings, and in conferences with students.

Chapter 12/Exercise 1
Answers will vary. Here are some possibilities.

1. finances	physical differences	hobbies	health
2. price	options/features	speed	exterior looks
3. profession	types of friends	money	lifestyle
4. free time	types of friends	finances	amount of sleep

Chapter 12/Exercise 2

Answers will vary

1. Another difference between dogs and cats is their energy level.
2. Secondly, dogs and cats need different types of care.
3. The third way that people who have pets are different from those who don't is health.
4. Another difference between types of snakes is that some are dangerous.
5. The final difference between people who are educated and those who are not is finances.
6. Another way that smokers differ from nonsmokers is their health.

Chapter 12/Exercise 3

Answers may vary.

I am going to tell you about the differences between high school in Haiti and college in the United States. Some differences are the time to finish a level, the language, and financial aid. First, in my country, high school students take one year to finish a level. For example, it took me one year to go from ninth grade to tenth grade, but in the United States, I can take three English language levels in one year. For example, I finished Beginning 1 English in one semester, Beginning 2 English in the second semester, and Intermediate 1 English in the third semester. This equals one year. Second, when I was in Haiti, I spoke Creole, but my teacher taught the class in French. However, in the United States, the teachers speak only English, and the students in our language program speak many different languages, such as Creole, Russian, Thai, and Spanish. Another big opportunity that the students in the United States have is financial aid, but in Haiti we don't have it at all. In conclusion, the success of schools depends on the government in all countries.

Chapter 12/Exercise 4

Answers will vary.